A Guide to the
Bodhisattva's Way of Life
of
Shantideva

Bibliotheca Indo-Buddhica Series no. 221

A Guide to the Bodhisattva's Way of Life of Shantideva

A Commentary

by

The Venerable Khenchen
Thrangu Rinpoche
Geshe Lharampa

Thrangu Rinpoche's Commentary
Translated by
Ken Holmes
Thomas Doctor

The Guide to a Bodhisattva's Life
Translated from the Sanskrit by
Marion Matics

Sri Satguru Publications
A Division of
Indian Books Centre
Delhi, India

Published by
Sri Satguru Publications,
Indological and Oriental Publishers
A Division of
Indian Books Centre
40/5, Shakti Nagar,
Delhi-110007
India

Email: ibcindia@vsnl.com
Website: http://www.indianbookscentre.com

First Indian Edition : Delhi, 2002

ISBN 81-7030-733-3

Acknowledgments

We would like to thank the persons who helped make this book
possible. First of all, we would like to thank Ken Holmes for translating
the teachings given in Nepal in 1987. We would also like to thank
Michael Connely, Margaret Neuman, and Susan Chapman for
transcribing the tapes.

We would like to thank Thomas Doktor for translating the teachings
given in 1995 in Nepal and Mimi Troilsi for transcribing these teachings.

Finally we would like to thank Eleanor Matics for allowing us to use
the excellent translation of Marion Matrics' translation of the root text.

Note

The technical words are italicized the first time they are used to alert
the reader that they can be found in the Glossary.

Tibetan and Sanskrit words are given as they are pronounced, not
spelled. For the Tibetan spelling see the Glossary of Tibetan Terms.

This book is a combination of teachings Thrangu Rinpoche gave in
1987 and in 1995 in Nepal. In each year he covered a different set of
chapters of this work.

Printed at Chawla Offset Printers, Delhi 110 052

Table of Contents

Shantideva

Foreword

As our Western civilization and now our Eastern counterparts become more and more materialistic, people of all countries, of all races, and all religions are looking for a meaning to their lives which is beyond mere material comfort and the accumulation of wealth. Some religions have looked towards a God or towards gods, while the Buddhist religion has looked towards the teachings of a most remarkable person who lived 500 years before Christ was born. The Buddha taught that there was only one way to achieve true happiness, that is complete and lasting freedom from suffering, and that is to achieve enlightenment.

So the question becomes how do we actually achieve this enlightenment? First of all, we must realize that achieving enlightenment relies completely upon ourselves. There is no external being or teacher who can give this to us. Second, we have to understand our mind and this is done by the techniques of meditation which are emphasized in the Theravada tradition. Third, we must also engage in impeccable behavior and this is emphasized in the Mahayana tradition.

One of the foremost texts of the Mahayana tradition is Shantideva's *A Guide to the Bodhisattva's Way of Life*. The story of Shantideva is quite interesting. Shantideva was a monk at Nalanda University just before it was destroyed by Moslem invasions. This vast monastic university had 10,000 individuals living together who did nothing other than study and practice the Buddhist dharma. Shantideva spent his time outwardly doing nothing and the story goes that his fellow monks decided to embarrass him by having him give a talk to the whole community. Shantideva took them up on this and gave the *Bodhisattva's Way of Life* which was the most brilliant commentary on how to engage on the Mahayana path to come out of Nalanda.

A bodhisattva is that Buddhist practitioner who has such incredible compassion for mankind that he or she has decided to help all other beings to reach enlightenment before him or herself.

The Bodhisattva's Life or *Bodhisattvacharyavatara* in Sanskrit is an enormously popular work and has been translated into dozens of languages. Unlike many Buddhist texts, this work has been preserved in both Sanskrit and in Tibetan and Chinese. The translation in various languages are very similar with only a few dozen verses being much different. There are four main translations of the root verses that are readily available in English.

First, there is Marion Matics pioneering work (New York: Macmillan Company, 1970) in which he translated the work from the Sanskrit. The Sanskrit is very similar to the Tibetan that Thrangu Rinpoche used for his commentary and this was the only translation which give us copyright permission to include in the text. This text is less literal and more poetical, but it conveys the meaning of the text quite well.

Second, there Stephen Batchelor's work *A Guide to the Bodhisattva's Way of Life*, Dharamsala, India: Library of Tibetan Works and Archives, 1979) in which he translated this work from the Tibetan. This was the translation that was used for the first set of teachings by Rinpoche's students in the 1987 teachings at the first Namo Buddha Seminar. The translation is good except for the famous ninth chapter on Wisdom in which Stephen Batchelor didn't simply translate the verses but added a commentary.

After Thrangu Rinpoche gave his commentary, the Padmakara Translation Group published *The Way of the Bodhisattva* (Boston: Shambhala Publications, 1997) which is more literal translation of the Tibetan text.

Finally, in that same year Vesna and Alan Wallace came out with *A Guide to the Bodhisattva Way of Life* (Ithaca, NY: Snow Lion Publications, 1997) which was based on both the Sanskrit and the Tibetan. What these translators did was translate the verses from the Sanskrit and whenever there were differences with the Tibetan they gave a translation of the Tibetan verse also.

These last two books are very readable and would be very helpful in understanding this text thoroughly. However, it must be remembered that Shantideva wrote this treatise for extremely erudite celibate monks who were very well versed in the extremely complex arguments of Madhyamaka logic. What Thrangu Rinpoche's commentary has to offer is that he has brought these teachings to be in accord with our modern Western society and the problems that his brings along with it. By combining the root text and also the commentary we hope to give the modern practitioner a valuable book to study.

Clark Johnson, Ph. D.

Chapter 1

The Benefits of an Awakened Mind

The Title

This book concerns the *Bodhisattva's Way of Life* by Shantideva[1] which in Sanskrit is the *Bodhisattva-charya-vatara*. The reason this text kept its name in Sanskrit is that it originated in India and was originally written in Sanskrit. The Tibetan title is *jang chub sem pay jod pa la jug pa*. The first part of the title *jang chub (kyi) sem* means "awakening mind" which is *bodhichitta* in Sanskrit. This awakening mind relates to the positive disposition of wanting to benefit others.[2]

There are many different degrees of such a mind. Even though we may have a good intention, when we actually carry out this intention, something harmful rather than beneficial results. In this text awakening mind refers to a positive mind which does not bring harm to others. So it's not ordinary goodness, but a very particular kind of awakening mind. Awakening mind has two qualities. The first quality is that one focuses on all sentient beings[3] without exception. Ordinary persons might be helpful towards their relatives and friends, but not towards those they don't like or enemies; some may help those of the same race, but not people of other races; and some may help human beings, but not animals. There are even those who are very loving towards cats and dogs, but not towards other animals such as spiders or snakes. However, the awakening mind focuses on all sentient beings without exception.

The second quality concerns the various ways one helps sentient beings. Some persons help others through curing their illnesses, others help other beings economically or materially. These kinds of help are good, but they are only temporary help. After some years this kind of help is gone, so ultimately it is of no great value.

The motivation of awakening mind is to help all sentient beings reach Buddhahood. This is something that will never deteriorate or be wasted. The Tibetan word for "awakening mind" is *jang chub kyi sem* and someone endowed with that mind is a *jang chub sem pa* or a *bodhisattva*. The last syllable *pa* refers to someone who is very courageous with respect to accomplishing the benefit for beings. So a bodhisattva is someone who doesn't become discouraged upon seeing the innumerable number of beings to be helped. A bodhisattva doesn't think, "I can't help all these beings; they're too numerous." A bodhisattva is also not discouraged realizing that it will take a very, very long time to aid and help all these sentient beings. A bodhisattva is also not discouraged by the many difficulties he or she has to undergo to help all beings. So a bodhisattva is very courageous with respect to helping all beings.

The final part of the title is (*jad pa la 'jug pa*) which means the way in which one enters or engages in a bodhisattva's deeds, or conduct or activities. Someone who is endowed with awakening mind is a bodhisattva which is a person who has developed goodness of mind. Just developing goodness of mind in itself is not sufficient because one has to know how to engage in the conduct of a bodhisattva. One begins by acquiring a knowledge of what a bodhisattva does and then one develops the understanding of how to engage in these deeds.

The Homage

The title of the *Bodhisattva's Way of Life* is followed by a homage to all the buddhas and bodhisattvas. This homage was written by the translators of the text. This book was actually translated three different times from Sanskrit into Tibetan: the first time was by the translator Kawa Paltseg (9th century C.E.); then by Rinchen Zangpo (958-1051 C.E.) and finally by Mo Lotsawa Loden Sherab. When the translators started a translation, they would start out by paying homage to all the buddhas and bodhisattvas to eliminate all hindrances or obstacles to the translation. In the Buddhist teachings there are what is termed the *Three Baskets* (Skt. *Tripitaka*): the *Abhidharma*, the *Sutras,* and the *Vinaya*. Translators would usually pay homage to Manjushri with a text related to the Abhidharma. In texts related to the Vinaya, the translator usually began paying homage to the omniscient Buddha. Texts related to the Sutras usually paid homage to all the buddhas and bodhisattvas. So we can see a *Guide to the Bodhisattva's Way of Life* belongs to the *sutra tradition*. From this point onward the text is Shantideva's words.

1.   *Bowing respectfully to the Buddhas, their sons, the dharma, and to all who*
     are praiseworthy, I will relate briefly, according to the Scriptures, the way
     that the offspring of the Buddhas enter the religious life.

The first verse is an offering of worship made by Shantideva. He follows a tradition which was followed by those who have composed the various different Buddhist texts. This verse was written for those who listen to the teachings that will be composed, those that explain the text, and those who practice what is being taught in the text. This is to induce faith and devotion for this outstanding persons who are all the buddhas and bodhisattvas.

2. *There is nothing really original here, and I have no skill in literary composition. I have composed this with no thought of any other purpose than to clarify my own mind.*

The verse offering worship is followed by a resolution to compose the text. Such a resolution is made by the author to write a perfect composition and to remind himself of the necessity of making a diligent and joyous effort while composing the text.

With these lines Shantideva is saying that what he is about to write down is not something that he has created himself, but something which is in accordance with the teachings of the Buddha. We may wonder about the need for commentaries on the teachings of the Buddha. The reason for commentaries is that the teachings of the Buddha are very vast. So to facilitate the practice and understanding for those of lesser intelligence, the author has decided to summarize some of the teachings of the Buddha to facilitate the practice and understanding for those with lesser grasp of the Buddha's teachings.

This verse was written to counteract arrogance and pride. Shantideva says that he himself has no special qualities and isn't very eloquent. Therefore, what he's about to write will probably not bring vast benefit to others. The reason he is writing this text is to acquaint himself to this awakening mind. This verse shows the necessity of counteracting arrogance and pride for himself personally and for those who will be listening to the teachings of the text, those who will be explaining the text, and those who will be practicing the teachings of the text. So this is like a quintessential instruction about the necessity of counteracting pride and arrogance.

3. *The pure impetus to become good is strengthened in me because of this effort; but if another person like myself should see it, may it be useful to him also.*

This verse was written to inspire practitioners and to induce inspiration for the deeds of the bodhisattvas. In the verse hopes that we will benefit from such conduct and that others will be benefited as well. If we practice these teachings, we will benefit others greatly. If we teach what has been written in the text to others, they will benefit greatly as well; therefore, these teachings are very meaningful. In this way the author exhorts himself and those that come in contact with this text to engage in the deeds of a bodhisattva.

An Outline of the Book

A *Guide to the Bodhisattva's Way of Life* consists of ten chapters. The first three chapters present the methods for giving rise to the awakening mind where it has not yet arisen; the last three chapters present the methods for guarding the awakening mind so that it does not deteriorate; and the following three chapters present methods to enable one to develop awakening mind. Then there is the tenth chapter, which dedicates all the virtue that has been accumulated for the happiness and welfare of all beings.

The first chapter of the *Bodhisattva's Guide* explains the benefits of the awakening mind. These benefits are given to induce inspiration for developing awakening mind. The second chapter teaches the way in which one should confess one's negative deeds, why one should confess, and so forth. If one's negative *karma* is purified, then the awakening mind will naturally arise. The third chapter is called the full acceptance of the awakening mind. At this point one makes vows to give rise to awakening mind.

The first chapter speaks of the benefits ensuing from engendering the awakening mind. In order to give rise to awakening mind, one needs what is termed a "superior body" which refers to a human body. For example, an animal has taken an inferior body; therefore the ability for engendering an awakening mind in an animal is non-existent because it is not possible for an animal to develop the awakening mind. So one needs the proper vessel or support to be able to give rise to the awakening mind. In addition to which, one needs to have developed goodness of mind. So that is why the following verse teaches:

4.   *This favorable moment, so hard to obtain, has arrived, leading to the achievement of man's well-being. If it is not utilized advantageously now, will the opportunity ever come again?*

We should without question make use of this present opportunity. The next verse relates to the motivation to practice the *dharma*. Such a motivation to practice the dharma is extremely rare.

5. *As lightning is seen brightly for an instant in the darkness of a clouded night, so perhaps, for once, the thought of the world may be turned, by the gesture of the Buddha, to good things for an instant.*

For example, at night when the moon is not shining and there is total darkness, and if there is a flash of lightening, we are able to see for a very brief moment. Similarly a mind continuously bent on achieving Buddhahood is very difficult to develop. The fact that it arises only once indicates that we are very, very fortunate. Even though it occurs for only a brief moment, we are very, very fortunate that it has occurred at all; since it is very, very rare that someone is continuously concerned with achieving Buddhahood.

The Training of a Bodhisattva

The training in the bodhisattva's way of life is a matter of gradual training. One gradually trains through reason. One first gains an understanding of why one practices. One then acquires an understanding of why one practices. One then acquires an understanding of the vast benefit that ensures for oneself and others. One develops understanding of this by developing the awakening mind and the result of suffering is avoided. If, on the other hand, one doesn't develop the awakening mind, suffering ensues both for oneself and others. So, by means of many logical arguments, the *Bodhisattva's Guide* points out why one is to practice and engage in this bodhisattva's way of life. Since the reasons for the practice is clear to one, there won't be a tendency to suppress one's own desires.

During the time of *Padmasambhava* (Tib. *Guru Rinpoche*) and the king *Thrisong Deutsen* in the ninth century there were three main Buddhist translators. Their short names were Ka, Shong, and Jya. The Ka refers to *Kawa Paltseg* who first translated the *Bodhisattva's Guide* into Tibetan. Then later on there was a Tibetan king *Langdarma* (ruled 901-906 C.E.) who destroyed the Buddhist teachings in Tibet. After that, *Rinchen Zangpo* (958-1051 C.E.) translated this text again into Tibetan because the previous translation had become corrupted during the time of Langdarma. Thereafter, Mo Lotsawa Loden Sherab who was a very great translator re-translated the text. *Tarthang Tulku* who presently lives in

Berkeley in the USA has the Dharma Publishing house which uses two emblems—a two-headed parrot and a two-headed duck. The two-headed parrot relates to the first two translators: Kawa Paltseg and Choro Lüi Gyeltsen. The two-headed duck refers to the first seven ordained monks in Tibet, two of which were outstanding and it is these two that these two-headed ducks represent. Since a duck is yellow, it represents ordination (a monk robes in Tibet has yellow in it) and represents these two outstanding members of the sangha in Tibet.

The Benefits of Awakening Mind

If one has a thorough knowledge of the benefits of awakening mind, one will naturally be inspired to develop the awakening mind. One doesn't have to push in order to do so. Knowing the benefits ensuing from having generated the awakening mind, then naturally without any effort, one will have great inspiration to do so.

6. *Indeed, goodness is weak, but the power of evil is always great and very dreadful. By what other goodness could evil be conquered if there were not surely the Awakening Mind?[4]*
7. *This benefit was discovered by the greatest sages after reflecting for many eons on the problem: Thus, happiness was heaped upon happiness, and happiness overflows to the immeasurable flood of humanity.*
8. *Never is the Awakening Mind to be relinquished by those who are desirous of escaping the hundreds of sorrows of existence, by those who are desirous of assuming the suffering of beings, or by those who are desirous of enjoying many hundreds of pleasures.*

Generally speaking, there are many methods to accumulate virtue. One can accumulate virtue through physical activity, verbal activity, or mental activity. The best of these different methods is engendering awakening mind. These verses show that awakening mind is the most outstanding method to accumulate virtue. Various beings have different desires: some want to eliminate suffering, some think of attaining happiness, some want to help others. The desire for awakening mind is indispensable because with awakening mind one is able to accumulate vast virtue. The consequence of accumulating vast virtue is that one is able to eliminate suffering. So awakening mind is then indispensable with respect to attaining whatever one desires.

In the past I have been asked why Buddhists speak of benefiting others, but do nothing on a practical level but emphasize meditation.

They say wouldn't it be preferable to look around and see what kind of help different persons need and give them money or clothes or something practical. Yes, on the spur of the moment this might seem true, but material goods benefit someone only temporarily. The main point of benefiting others is to have a stable and firm motivation. If one lacks such a motivation, the benefit to others might not ensure making only a slight, temporary benefit. Whereas a very stable and firm motivation to benefit others is preferable. So therefore one should try to increase such a steady and complete motivation.

9. The wretched one who is bound by the fetters of existence instantly is proclaimed a son of the Buddhas. He becomes worthy of being praised in the worlds of men and of immortals when the Awakening Mind has arisen.

An individual who has not yet given rise to the awakening mind is term an "ordinary being." An ordinary being is concerned with his or her own welfare and therefore wanders and is fettered in *conditioned existence* (Skt. *samsara*). Once we have given rise to the awakening mind, we are a bodhisattva. Awakening mind is very powerful and great benefits ensue. So once the awakening mind has arisen, we become a bodhisattva or a "son of the *sugata*.[5]" Our activity will become more meaningful, since awakening mind is very powerful. Because of this we are worthy of respect by both men and gods of the world.

Analogies for Awakening Mind

10. Having overpowered this impure likeness of one's self, one should create the priceless likeness of a Conqueror's jewel. Seize firmly that very lively elixir which is the concept of Enlightenment.

Shantideva now begins to explain awakening mind through five different analogies. The first analogy comes from alchemy in particular a substance called the philosophers' stone[6] which is able to turn iron into gold. By means of this stone one is able to transform an inferior substance into a superior one. This analogy describes the necessity of becoming enlightened. Presently, we are ordinary beings and we need to transform ourselves into buddhas.

This is done by firmly accepting and developing awakening mind. So developing awakening mind is like the philosophers' stone.

*11. You who are accustomed to dwelling abroad in the marketplaces of destiny,
seize firmly that highly priced jewel, the Awakening Mind, so well-attested
by those of immeasurable thought, the unique leaders of the world's
caravan.*

In the second analogy, awakening mind is compared to a precious jewel.
In the old days merchants who bought and sold jewels would cross great
oceans to find a place where there were a lot of jewels. Often these
merchants depended on a guide who had previously crossed the oceans
and found the jewels. The analogy then is the Buddha who is called "the
sole guide of the world" (the *bhagavan*) who first found these precious
jewels, that is, the awakening mind. After discovering these jewels, he
showed them to us. So in the same way as a merchant finds jewels and
carefully takes care of these jewels, we should firmly find and take hold
of this precious awakening mind.

*12. All other goodness, having lost its fruit, like the banana tree, begins to
decay: But that tree which is the Awakening Mind begets and does not
decay. It bears fruit perpetually.*

In the third analogy awakening mind is compared to a plantain tree. A
banana tree bears fruit only after the trunk of the tree dries up and
perishes. This is comparable to virtue that has been accumulated which
lacks the motivation of the awakening mind. When this happens, the
virtue perishes. On the other hand, there are perennial trees which bear
fruit every year and the fruit usually grows bigger and bigger. Since
virtue that has been accumulated out of the awakening mind will increase
constantly until one has attained Buddhahood, this virtue is never wasted
and flourishes without end.

*13. Whoever has committed the most dreadful evil may escape at once by taking
refuge, as one escapes great dangers by taking refuge under the protection
of a hero. Why is this refuge not taken by ignorant beings?*

The fourth analogy compares awakening mind to entrusting ourselves to
a brave person. If we are afraid of something and combat this fear by
entrusting ourselves to a brave person or bodyguard who, for example,
has a weapon that can protect us, we can proceed without fearing anyone
or anything. In the same way, if we have engendered the awakening
mind then we don't need to fear the effects of the evils that we have
committed. So if we entrust ourselves to the awakening mind, then we

don't need to fear anything.

14. *Like the time of fire at the end of a world cycle, it instantly consumes the greatest evils; its immeasurable benefits were taught to [the disciple] Sudhana by the wise Lord Maitreya.*

The fifth analogy is of the hell fire which is said to come at the end of our eon (Skt. *kalpa*). So here it is taught that if we have engendered the awakening mind, then immediately all evil one has accumulated will be eliminated. If we, for example, have some paper and lights it, the paper will burn up immediately. Similarly, the awakening mind will instantly consume all evils that we have accumulated.

The text mentions five analogies but there are actually many other analogies as well. Shantideva stops at these five analogies and continues saying that there are other examples in the sutras. One in particular is the sutra called the *Gandavyuha* sutra. One can look up different analogies in other texts. Shantideva mentions five and then goes on to say that other explanations can be found in other texts.

The Two Aspects of Awakening Mind

15. *This Awakening Mind is to be understood as twofold. Briefly, it is the idea of dedication to Enlightenment (bodhi-pranidhi-chitta) and then the actual pilgrimage towards it (bodhi-prasthana).*
16. *As concisely stated by learned men, this difference is that between a traveler and someone desirous of traveling.*

There are two kind of awakening mind: the mind that aspires to awaken (relative bodhichitta) and the mind that actually does so (absolute bodhichitta). The first kind is similar to desiring to go to a place and the second kind is similar to actually going to the desired destination. The first aspect or kind of awakening mind is the desire to benefit sentient beings and the second aspect is the actual practice of helping them. The benefit of beings is accomplished by meditating on the awakening mind and practicing the *six perfections* (Skt. *paramitas*). We may wonder what benefits ensue from these two aspects. The text therefore goes on to explain these benefits.

17. *The idea of dedication to Enlightenment brings great fruit even on the wheel of rebirth (samsara), but not the uninterrupted meritoriousness of the mind which is set upon departure.*

The first aspect of aspiring awakening mind results in benefits; but, the benefits ensuing from the venturing mind that actually practices awakening mind is greater. The text says:

18. *As soon as one undertakes to free himself from the unbounded realms of living beings, he concentrates his mind (citta) with steadfast thought;*
19. *that soon, in spite of sleep and repeated excitement, floods of merit, equal to the sky, begin to flow without ceasing.*

Once we have given rise to the accomplished wakening mind, then from that time onward there will always be benefits even if one is asleep or unconcerned.

We may now wonder who has said that great virtue and benefits ensue from cultivating awakening mind. How can we know that this is really the case. Actually, we can find this out in the teachings of the Buddha in various sutras. We may also wonder why the Buddha taught these teachings. The reason is that these teachings help overcome the fear of developing the awakening mind. Certain practitioners may fear such an approach of trying to enlighten all sentient beings. So for our benefit the Buddha taught about the great virtues ensuing from giving rise to the awakening mind, particularly, the second aspect of awakening mind. To understand these teachings given by the Buddha, we depend on scriptural authority and on logical reasoning. The next verse is concerned with scriptural authority:

20. *This the Buddha himself correctly has asserted in the [scripture] Subahupriccha for the sake of beings of lesser aspiration.*

The next two verses establish the benefits of the awakening mind by means of reasoning:

21. *One who is a kindly benefactor thinks, "I will cure the headaches of beings." Thus by this benevolent intention he has acquired immeasurable merit.*
22. *How much more to wish to remove the infinite ache of every single being and for each one to create infinite virtue!*

These two verses are concerned with the first aspiration for awakening mind. From this aspiration infinite goodness ensues.

There is a story in relation to this. Once upon a time there was a merchant called Sawo Phumo who had many children who were all sons. All his sons, however, died. To prevent the death of his latest born son, he gave him a girl's name thinking that would prevent the boy's death. This boy was generally a very good person; being very good to his mother and so forth. One day though, this boy decided to go and find jewels. His mother became very upset fearing he would die. She begged him not to go saying, "you will die on the road." The boy became very upset and angry with her and kicked her in the head and left. As a result of being a very good person, he found a lot of good jewels on his first voyage. He crossed a great ocean and came to an island where he found a lot of beautiful jewels. He then wanted to the south but everyone warned him not to go there. But he decided to go south anyway and continued until he came to another island where he found a house made of iron. He became curious and went into the house. In the house he found a man who had a iron wheel turning in his head causing great pain. So this boy asked how this had happened and the man who was suffering answered, "It is because I kicked my mother in the head once and this is the result of having done so." At that point, the same thing happened to the boy. But rather than being bitter at this misfortune, he thought of all the sentient being that suffered and he developed the desire to relieve them of that suffering. The moment the genuine desire to relieve all sentient being of suffering arose in his mind, the iron wheel stopped turning in his head and rose into the air.

So we see from this story that the boy's beneficial intention had an immediate effect by relieving his suffering instantly. With respect to awakening mind, we shouldn't be concerned only with beings that suffer in a specific way, but be concerned with the suffering of all sentient beings. There are, of course, an inconceivable number of sentient beings and we should be concerned about all of them.

The Greatness of Awakening Mind

The next verses explain that the awakening mind and bodhisattva practice can dispel all suffering of sentient beings. So the benefits ensuing from the first aspect of aspiring awakening mind results in indescribable benefits.

23. *Whose mother or father is endowed with this benevolent desire? To what gods or sages or Brahmans does it belong?*

24. *Even in sleep this desire has not previously arisen for these people, not even in self-interest: How much less its appearance for the sake of others?*

25. *This unprecedented, distinctive jewel among beings: How is it given birth? This intention which is for the welfare of others does not appear in others*

even in self-interest.
26. *This merit-of the seed of the world's joy, of the medicine for the world's sorrow, of the jewel of the mind: How, indeed, may it be measured?*

So not even the love that fathers and mothers have for their children have such a beneficial intention as a bodhisattva. Since bodhisattvas have engendered the awakening mind and this ends the suffering of all beings. Bodhichitta is, then, the cause which relieves beings of their pain.

The ensuing verses explain the benefits from the second aspect of accomplishing awakening mind which is making the actual effort of benefiting all beings without exception.

27. *The worship of Buddhas is excelled by merely having a desire for goodness: How much more by zeal for the total welfare of all beings?*
28. *Yet some rush to sorrow only because of the hope of escaping sorrow. Although striving for happiness, like their own enemy, they stupidly destroy their own happiness.*
29. *The one who bestows the satisfaction of all pleasure cuts off the afflictions of those who are avaricious for pleasure*
30. *and thus constantly afflicted; so and, likewise, he destroys confusion. What goodness is comparable to his? Where is there such a friend or such merit as this?*

The following verses continue in the same way describing the benefits ensuing from developing the second aspect of the awakening mind established by means of reasoning. The verses are:

31. *Truly, whoever reciprocates for a service rendered is highly praised; but what can be said of a Bodhisattva who is not concerned with his own good?*
32. *The one who gives a feast for a few men is honored by men, who say that he is a doer of good, because he proudly supports life for half a day by giving a brief measure of food.*
33. *What of the one who gives in limitless time to a limit- less number of beings that full satisfaction of total desire which is imperishable even when the inhabitants of heaven perish?*

So there are those individuals that give food to poor people which gives them a full stomach for only half a day, but these people don't feel any respect for the beggar. Such a patron is then honored as a very virtuous and generous person, even though in comparison to a bodhisattva, a patron does very little. A bodhisattva, however, engages him or herself in activity that results in the complete happiness of Buddhahood which results in fulfilling all the hopes of sentient beings.

The Qualities of a Bodhisattva

The qualities of an individual who has engendered the awakening mind
are explained as follows:

34. *Indeed, whoever conceives evil in his heart against the Lord of the Feast,
the son of the Conqueror, he will dwell for eons in hell, because of the
reckoning up of evil interest. So spoke the Lord.*
35. *But he whose mind is turned to tranquillity will produce fruit which is
superior to it; for, certainly, an act of evil requires great strength, but
goodness to the sons of the Conqueror is without effort.*
36. *I reverence their bodies, wherein this most excellent jewel of the mind has
arisen, wherein even a sin results in happiness. I go for refuge to these
resources of happiness.*

The text says that one should venerate and respect a bodhisattva, since
such an individual is an outstanding person and has out-standing
qualities. One should, therefore, respect a bodhisattva and take refuge in
him or her.

This concludes the first chapter of *A Guide to a Bodhisattva's Way
of Life* which has explained the benefits of bodhichitta or awakening
mind. The reason for this explanation is that we need knowledge of these
benefits to be able to raise awakening mind or bodhichitta. We won't be
able to engender these attitudes just by thinking, "I will do it." We need
some inspiration to do so and this inspiration can be drawn from the
knowledge of the benefits ensuing from the awakening mind. We will
feel inspired to give rise to the awakening mind. So the first chapter
begins by explaining the benefits giving rise to awakening mind, then it
explains the benefits ensuing from the two aspects of awakening mind
and finally it explains the outstanding qualities of a bodhisattva that has
already developed the awakening mind.

Questions

Question: Why can't gods, sages, and Brahmin reach enlightenment?
Rinpoche: The gods, sages, and Brahmin are only concerned with their
own welfare. They practice to attain Buddhahood only to eliminate their
personal suffering. Therefore they have never even dreamt of an attitude

of awakening mind being concerned only with their own welfare.
Question: Could you explain further the fear of a bodhisattva faced with the task of helping absolutely all sentient beings?
Rinpoche: The fear of engendering awakening mind is thinking, "Well, I'll never be able to help all these beings, since they are so numerous." One thinks of all these numerous and various beings and all their desires and that one is not able to fulfill all their hopes and desires. So there is a fear of engendering the awakening mind or engaging in bodhisattva activity.

It might seem that this effort involves suffering, but it also involves happiness. For example, if you are concerned about ten people and you help one of them, then you feel very happy. You will be content with your effort of having been able to help one person. So if you are able to help two or three or more of these people, you will be even more happy. So in the case of a bodhisattva who is concerned with a limitless number of beings, the bodhisattva's happiness and joy is continuous. It is continuous because the bodhisattva is concerned with the welfare of so many and each time someone is helped, the bodhisattva is happy. So, in fact, there is a continuous happiness and joy, rather than suffering with this commitment.

Question: How much negative karma is erased from doing good actions?
Rinpoche: The virtue resulting from giving rise to the awakening mind is very powerful. In fact, it consumes negative karma. In the case of extremely strong negative karma, awakening mind will, so to speak, take away the effect, though one will have to experience some of the effects of this negative karma. In the case of a slight misdeed, it will be eliminated totally by awakening mind. If one, for example, has accumulated karma which will result in rebirth in hell and after one has given rise to the awakening mind, the future effect of this negative karma will be very slight. For example, if you drop a ball, it bounces back off the ground. In the same way, rather than having to dwell in the hell realms for a very long period of time, one might just fall down into the hell realms and then bounce up again like a ball.

Chapter 2

The Confession of Negative Deeds

The second chapter on confession of negative deeds is divided into four parts: offerings, homage (or prostrations), refuge, and confession.

To engender the aspiration for awakening mind it is necessary to counteract hindrances and unfavorable conditions. The best method to eliminating these hindrances and unfavorable conditions is the accumulation of merit. The best method to accumulate merit is to practice the *seven branches*. The first four of the seven branches is discussed in this second chapter.

The first branch is the making of offerings. We make offerings to reverse or counteract the *disturbing emotions* (Skt. *klesha*) of attachment. There are different types of offerings. The first type is material offerings of things we own. The second type are mental offerings that we don't own such as a beautiful mountain, or a beautiful river, or a forest. We mentally offer all these pure and beautiful things. The third type of offering is offering our body.

1. Making Offerings

1. In order to grasp this jewel of the mind, I offer worship to the Buddhas, and to the spotless jewel of the true Dharma, and to the sons of the Buddha, who are oceans of virtue:

The chapter starts out with the first offering of material objects that we are actually able to gather together such as bathing water, pure drinking water, flowers, incense, and foods. To be able to seize this precious awakening mind we make these offerings to the *three rare and supreme jewels* (the Buddha, the dharma, and the *sangha*).

The reason for making these offerings is to generate the awakening mind. It is very important to know that the awakening mind is very outstanding, excellent, and very important. Second, we should then realize that the buddhas, the sangha, and the dharma that all teach the awakening mind are also not ordinary; but are endowed with outstanding qualities. We should feel from the depths of our heart that these are excellent and outstanding, and then we make offerings. So if we have, for example, two bracelets—one made of brass and one made of gold, we wouldn't consider the iron ornament very precious and have any particular attachment to it; whereas the golden. bracelet would be considered very precious and we would have great desire for it. Similarly, we shouldn't consider the three rare and supreme ones as ordinary like and brass ornament, but should relate to them as being like a gold ornament. We should understand, feel, and realize that they are outstanding, endowed with great qualities, and so forth and for this reason we should make the supreme offerings to them.

Material Offerings

2. *As many flowers and fruits and species of healing herbs as exist in the world, and as many jewels as exist, and waters clear and refreshing;*

3. *likewise, mountains of jewels, and forest places to be enjoyed in solitude, and vines blazing with flower-decoration, and trees whose branches bow down with good fruit;*

4. *and in the world of gods and the like, fragrant incenses; wish-fulfilling trees, and trees of jewels;[7] lakes adorned with lotuses, and the endlessly fascinating cry of wild geese;*

5. *harvests without cultivation, and crops of grain, and everything else ornamenting those worthy of worship; things within the limits of extended space and likewise all things which belong to no one.*

6. *These I offer mentally to the eminent sages (muni) and to their little sons. May the great Compassionate Ones, worthy of choice gifts, mercifully accept this from me.*

7. *I have nothing else for worship. Therefore, for my sake, let the Lords whose highest object is the mind), accept this through my own effort.*

These verses give examples of mental offerings of things we don't own such as pure water, gem-encrusted mountains, quiet forests, fruit-laden trees, or anything else that's pure and precious. We don't offer these things to the three jewels because the Buddha, dharma, or sangha desire the offerings. The reason we make these offerings is to engender aspiration, faith, devotion, accumulation of merit, and so forth. So whether we are able to gather together material offerings or is only able to mentally offer pure and precious substances, the accumulation of merit will ensure. So whether we are able to gather material offerings or not is not the main point. Instead we can make mental offerings such as those mentioned in the text.

Offerings of Body

The third type of offering is our own body. We should then try to offer whatever is very important to us—whatever we are attached to the most of all. In fact what we grasp onto most of all is our own body and we consider this very important. When we make an offering of something which we are attached to a great deal, we accumulate greater merit. So the greater the grasping of what is being offered, the greater the merit accumulated.

8. *And I give myself to the Conquerors completely, and to their sons. Pre-eminent Beings take possession of me! Through devotion I go into servitude.*
9. *By your taking possession of me I become without fear of existence, I do good to all beings, and I by-pass former sin, and, moreover, I do no further sin.*

These verses were concerned with offering our body to the three rare and supreme ones. So this should not just be mere lip service; it should have some actual meaning, and it should be put into practice. The sentence "respectfully shall I be your subject" means that we commit ourselves to being the servant of the three rare and supreme ones. This doesn't mean that we just give them food, help clean their house and so forth. Rather it means that we "no more fears conditioned existence" which is to say, we will others instead of fearing conditioned existence. This is done by confessing negative activities so that we then accumulate virtue and then practice virtue. In this way we accumulate merit and are able to help others. It is in this way that we are able to please that rare and supreme ones.

Mental Offerings

We now come to the mentally imagined objects. We imagine or visualize offering bathing water, various cloths, clothes, and ornaments in the following part.

10. *In their houses of perfumed bathing, with delightful pillars of blazing jewels, with canopies shining with pearls, with their mosaic pavements brilliant and clear,*
11. *I myself will prepare the bath of the Buddhas and their sons, with the playing of songs, using many water jars encrusted with great jewels and filled with flowers and fragrant waters agreeable to the mind.*
12. *With garments perfumed, purified of dirt, unequaled, I dry their bodies.*

Then I give them well-colored, well- perfumed, choice robes.

13. *With celestial, delicate, smooth, varied, handsome garments, with choice ornaments; with such as these I adorn Samantabhadra, Ajita, Mafijughosha, Lokekvara, and the rest.*

14. *With the perfumes which pervade all of the three thousand worlds, with the uttermost perfumes, I anoint the bodies of all the great sages, who shine with a radiance like well-refined, well-polished, and well-cleaned gold.*

The text goes on to speak of offerings of land, palaces, and precious umbrellas. These things are mentally created and offered. We cannot actually gather these objects and offer them on a material level because they don't actually exist; so it's a question of mental offerings. We accumulate merit as a result of these mental offerings and this is done in order to engender the awakening mind.

We make an offering of pleasing and beautiful piece of land. Then we make the offering of palaces and then we offer precious umbrellas.

15. *With the blossoms of the coral tree, the blue lotus, jasmine, and the like; with all perfumed and delightful flowers, I praise the most praiseworthy best of sages with beautifully formed garlands.*

16. *I envelop them with clouds of incense, delighting the mind with dense, expanding aromas; and I offer to them an offering of various moist and dry foods and libations.*

17. *I offer them jewel lamps placed in rows on golden lotuses; and on mosaic pavements anointed with perfume I scatter many pleasing flowers.*

18. *Celestial clouds delightful as songs of praise, ornamenting the four directions, shining as garlands of gems and pearl necklaces: These also I offer to the Benevolent Ones.*

19. *I place before those who are the great sages lofty jewel parasols encrusted with pearls, exceedingly handsome, with pleasingly shaped golden handles.*

Offering Aspirational Prayers

The following verses are concerned with offering aspirational prayers. An aspirational prayer cannot be collected on a material level, nor is it unowned, nor can we create a mental image of it. These are just aspirational prayers. We pray for specific things which pleases the three rare and supreme ones and these prayers are an offering in itself. The verses are as follows:

20. *Hereafter may delightful clouds of worship) arise, and clouds of music and song which thrill all creatures.*

21. Upon all jewels of the true Dharma, shrines, and images, may the rains of flowers, jewels, and such, fall without end.

The next offering is called the incomparable offering. It is concerned with offerings made by outstanding beings, such as *Manjughosha*. These outstanding individuals having attained the *bodhisattva levels*, made offerings to accumulate merit. We don't really know how they did this, but we imagine that we offer in the same incomparable way as they did. This is in the following verse:

22. Manjughosa and the others worship the Conquerors, thus I worship the Lord Buddhas and their sons;

In the next verse, we offer praise to these excellent beings. This offering is not made on a material level. We praise the qualities of these excellent beings so that our faith, devotion, and respect will increase.

23. I praise with hymns, with oceans of sound, these Seas of Virtue. Let clouds of singing praise unfailingly arise to them.

2. Offering Homage or Prostrations

The second section of the chapter on confession is concerned with the branch of prostrations or homage which is an antidote for pride. When a practitioner of the dharma begins to think of him or herself as equal to or superior to his or her teacher, then that individual won't be able to develop any positive qualities. It is pride that prevents good qualities from arising. An analogy is if you have a hollow vessel, you are able to pour water into it and it will retain the water. Whereas, if you have a lump of something, no matter how much water you pour onto it, no water will be retained. In the same way, pride prevents one from developing and retaining qualities.

24. With salutations as numerous as the atoms in all Buddha-fields, I salute the Buddhas of all three worlds (of past, present, and future) and the Dharma, and the great congregations.
25. Likewise, I praise all shrines and places associated with Bodhisattvas; and I make obeisance to praiseworthy teachers and ascetics.

When making this offering which is often called paying homage, one folds one's hands. The five fingers in each hand shouldn't be spread apart. There should also be a proper mental attitude; one should be filled with respect for those that one prostrates to. One then pays respect through body by touching one's folded hands at the forehead (or sometimes at the top of one's head). Then one folds one's hands at the level of the throat to symbolize respect of speech. Finally, one places one's folded hands at the level of the throat to symbolize respect of speech. Finally, one places one's folded hands at the heart to symbolize mental respect.[8] So in this way we pay respect to the three and rare and supreme ones through body, speech, and mind. We should realize that we are not in any way equal to the person we are making prostrations to. We should rather realize that we are inferior to the objects of our homage. So without any pride whatsoever we should make these prostrations by touching five points to the ground: the forehead, the two hands, and the two knees. We do this because we understand that they have outstanding qualities and we have no such qualities; but we need to attain such qualities in the future.

The line "I praise all shrines and places associated with bodhichitta" refers to the places where the awakening mind has been aroused by great beings in the past. For example, in *Bodh Gaya* where the Buddha turned the *wheel of dharma* (Skt. *dharmachakra*) for the first time, there are many such holy places that have been blessed by great beings of the past. We have the Swayambhu *stupa* in Kathmandu which has been blessed by *Manjushri* and we have the Bodhanath *stupa* which is also in Nepal and has been blessed by Padmasambhava, King *Trisong Detsen*, and Khunchen Shivatsur. They have blessed this place and made aspirational prayers here, so we pay homage to such places.

3. Taking Refuge

Taking refuge is the third branch of homage. In terms of the Hinayana or lesser vehicle, one takes refuge for this life lasting until one dies. But in terms of the Mahayana or greater vehicle, one takes refuge until one has attained Buddhahood. The text says:

26. I seek refuge in all buddhas
Until I possess the essence of Awakening,
Likewise I seek refuge in dharma
And in the assembly of Bodhisattvas

4. The Branch of Confession

The fourth part of confessing negative deeds is actually making a confession. To begin with, the Buddhist tradition holds the view that some beings are happy and some suffer. Whether they suffer or not depends upon whether they have accumulated either good or bad karma in the past. One's past karma is the cause of or is responsible for one's present condition and is therefore responsible for whether one is happy or not. The law of cause and effect, that is, the law of karma, is infallible. If one has accumulated good karma, one will for certain experience a pleasant result. If one has accumulated bad karma, for certain the result will be suffering. So we have to confess negative actions to prevent the negative effect of suffering.

There is a method of confession or disclosure of negative actions by which one purifies negative karma committed in the past. For confession one needs to first recognize the negative karma; one needs to regret what bad deeds one has done, and one needs to promise not to commit any such actions again. If one confesses with this understanding, the confession will result in the purification of the negative karma that was accumulated.

There are two parts to the confession: the object of the confession (the negative action) and the actual act of confessing.

27. With folded hands, I implore the perfect Buddhas stationed in all places, and likewise the great compassionate Bodhisattvas:

We first bring to mind those to whom we confess, that is, all the buddhas and bodhisattvas that reside in all the ten directions and have compassion for sentient beings.

When we confess, we think of the *four remedial powers* to mind and then confesses. The first remedial power is recognizing the faults that ensue from having committed the negative karma and the recognition that we will eventually experience an unpleasant result. We believe that we do not benefit in any way by this negative karma and, in fact, we are harmed by it. Others are also harmed by it. So by recognizing the faults ensuing from negative karma, we will develop a dislike for such action, which is the first remedial power covered in the following verses:

28. Whatever evil, on the endless wheel of rebirth (samsara),
29. simply right here, whatever evil was committed by me, an animal, or caused to be committed, and whatever was enjoyed foolishly, ending in self-

destruction, that evil I confess, stricken with remorseful feeling.

30. Whatever wrong I have done to the three Jewels, or to my mother and father, or to praiseworthy teachers, by abuse of deed, speech or thought;

31. by many dark offenses, by the evil wrought by me, Lords, whatever violent evil was done—all that I confess.

32. How can I escape from it? I am eternally fearful, Lords. Let death not be soon, because of my despair that my evil has not diminished.

33. How can I escape from it? Rescue me with haste! Death will come quickly and my evil has not diminished.

34. This death is not considerate of what has been done or not done: a great, sudden thunderbolt, the killer as we rest, distrusted by the healthy and by the sick.

35. For the sake of that which is dear and of that which is not dear, I have done evil in various ways. I did not understand that all which has been done must be relinquished.

36. That which is not dear to me will not be; that which is dear to me will not be; and I will not be; and all will not be.

37. Whatever reality is experienced, it becomes like a thing remembered. Like a dream-experience all has gone and is not seen again.

38. Many who were here just for a moment have died, whether good or bad, yet the evil caused by them remains present and terrible.

39. I did not consider that I also am such a stranger. Be cause of confusion, attachment, and hatred, I have frequently done evil.

40. Night and day, incessantly, the decay of life increases; and there is no help coming. Shall I not surely die?

41. The agony of intense pain, whether accompanied by family or by myself in my bed, must be endured alone.

42. When one is seized by the envoys of death, what value is a relative? What value is a friend? At that moment, merit is the only protection, and that was never attended to by me.

43. Because of attachment to my transient life, by ignorance of this fearful prospect, by foolishness, Lords, I have acquired much evil.

44. The one who even today is carried off for the sake of a mere amputation withers away; he is thirsty, his sight is afflicted, he sees the world other [than it is].

45. How much more when one has been overcome by the formidable messengers of death, seized by the fever of great fear, wound about with filth and excrement?

46. With despair, and with eyes directed to the four quarters, I look for protection. What ascetic (sadhu) will be my protector [and deliver me] from this great fear?

47. Having seen all quarters devoid of protection, and having fallen again into complete confusion, what then shall I do in that place of great fear?

The first remedial power is that it is important to recognize the faults and defects that ensue from negative actions. There are various ways in which we can meditate with respect to this first remedial power. Generally we should meditate on that all phenomena are impermanent. Then we should contemplate why we engage in accumulating negative karma. At times, we do negative actions to help friends and at other times we do negative actions to get back at people we don't like. We should then consider the results ensuing from these various activities. In fact, we are not really able to benefit friends and relatives because the life of beings is not very long, not much longer than 60 or 70 years. It would be good, of course, if we were able to help them for maybe two or three hundred years. But in fact, we aren't able to do so since no one lives that long.

On the other hand, the life span of people who have harmed us is also short, so we are not really able to harm them. We are not really able to benefit our friends and relatives, and not really able to harm our enemies. The life span of beings is short so the ensuing result of this negative karma accumulated is that we are harmed, we haven't been able to benefit those we desired to benefit, and we haven't been able really to harm those we wanted to harm. We have harmed ourselves, in fact, since the result from these actions will ripen and we will come to experience these results in the future which results in suffering. So negative actions or karma is rather meaningless, since we are not able to attain the goals we have set up.

So the first "remedial power" is recognizing negative karma and the ensuing results. As was said we are not able to benefit close ones, nor are we able to harm enemies. Therefore such activity is meaningless. We should understand this and we should also understand also that we are greatly harmed by such actions since the effects will ripen in us in the future causing future suffering. So we should understand that such negative actions are in fact meaningless, and that we will be greatly harmed by them, experiencing the future results that is a variety of suffering. By understanding this, we should develop a dislike for evil actions. Such dislike will naturally counteract the effect of negative karma for the future.

The second remedial power is concerned with the object of one's confession. Once we understand that negative actions that ensue are the root of us being harmed. Therefore we need to confess these evil actions. The object of our confession should be outstanding or exalted. We make this confession in the presence of the Buddha and all great bodhisattvas such as *Manjushri*, *Vajrapani*, and *Vajradhara* and so forth. We confess in their presence, beseeching them to eliminate the unpleasant results of the ripening of our negative karma. This is the second remedial power:

48. *Therefore, I go now for refuge to the Lords of the earth, the ones laboring for the sake of the earth's protection, the Conquerors who dispel all fear; and likewise I go for refuge to the Dharma that is mastered by them, which consumes the fear of rebirth: and I go to the company of Bodhisattvas.*
49. *Trembling with fear, I give myself to Samantabhadra, and again I give myself, by my own action, to Manjughosha;*
50. *and to the Lord Avalokita, who is entirely occupied with the practice of compassion, I, who am terrified, cry aloud a cry of suffering, "May he protect me, a sinner!"*
51. *the noble kfiagarbha and to Ksitigarbha, and indeed to all the great Compassionate Beings, I cry aloud, looking for protection.*
52. *And I worship the Lord of the Thunderbolt. When they have seen him, the messengers of death and the other evil beings are frightened and they flee to the four directions.*
53. *I now go terrified to you for refuge—after having neglected your instruction, because of beholding fear. May you quickly extinguish fear.*

Here we beseech the Buddha and all great bodhisattvas such as Samantrabhadra, Manjushri, Vajradhara, Vajrapani and request them to eradicate the future result ensuing from our negative karma.

So with this second remedial power of support of the first remedial power which understands that unvirtue brings about suffering, v e will develop some fear for the result of these actions. At this point we need a refuge and this is the three rare and supreme ones, along with all the great bodhisattvas. That is the second remedial power of support.

The third remedial power is to engage in remedial powers, that is to say, in the practice of the accumulation of virtue. We turn to the three rare and supreme ones along with all great bodhisattvas, requesting them to clear away or eliminate the effect of the future effects of the evil karma or actions that one has accumulated. At this point, we may wonder whether the three rare and supreme ones and all great bodhisattvas are able to immediately clear away these future results. The answer is "no." They can't do this because we have committed and accumulated these negative actions, not them. Therefore they don't have the power to immediately clear away these future results. The three rare and supreme ones and all great bodhisattvas have great compassion for all sentient beings, so if they were able to eliminate these unpleasant future results, they would do so. But since it is us who has committed these negative actions, they can't. It does, however, help to pray to them and to request their help because if we develop faith and devotion for these great beings, then they will show one the path and method that will allow us to eliminate the fruition of our negative karma. So it is our personal effort that we are able to clear away these future effects of karma. By developing faith and devotion and then following the path shown to us, we are able to purify our negative karma. The method for purifying our negative actions is to accumulate virtue and practice virtue.

The third remedial power concerns why and how we rely on these powers has two aspects to it: the reason why it is necessary to rely upon these powers, and the way in which one does this:

54. *Dreading even a passing disease, one would not violate the command of a physician. Why, then, after being ravaged by four hundred and four diseases?*

55. *Yet all men dwelling in Jambudvipa [our continent] perish because of even a single disease for which no medicine is found.*

56. *Because I violate the command of the all-knowing Physician, the one who in such a case takes away all cause of pain, shameful is my complete confusion!*

57. *I will stand with extreme care upon any other precipice; why not, then, upon that precipice which is a thousand worlds in depth and of immense duration?*

58. *Perhaps death does not come today, but nonetheless I ought not to be at ease; inevitably the hour comes when I shall not exist.*

59. *By whom is security given to me? and how shall I escape? Inevitably I shall not exist. How can the mind be composed?*

60. *What lasting value survives from the vanished experience of an earlier day? What remains to me when I have neglected the word of the gurus?*

61. *Having forsaken this land of the living, with its relatives and friends, I shall go somewhere all alone. What to me is all that is dear or not dear?*

62. *This thought is with me always, night and day, sorrow is caused by the evil deed. How then can I escape?*

With respect to the first part of the third power, the text explains the reason why we have to rely upon these powers. This is done using two analogies. The first is that if one is stricken by a disease and one needs to follow the doctor's advice, otherwise one will not be able to cure the disease and become well. Similarly, we need to practice the methods that are given by the Buddha and great bodhisattvas to purify our negative actions or karma. There is no other method to purify our negative karma. Therefore we need to follow these great beings' advice as we would follow the advice of our doctor.

The second analogy is of a precipice which illustrates that we have to be very conscientious with respect to negative actions or karma. We need to carefully avoid such actions. If we are at the edge of a very small precipice we would be careful so that we don't fall. Similarly, we should be very careful and conscientious with respect to negative actions, otherwise we will experience suffering for a very, very long time. Therefore, we should continuously be conscientious and careful with respect to negative karma and avoid such actions.

The following two verses are then concerned with the second analogy:

63. *Whatever the evil which has been accumulated by my foolishness and ignorance, and whatever of my speaking and teaching is objectionable, and whatever is evil by nature:*
64. *I confess it all, standing in the presence of the Lords, fearing sorrow, and with folded hands prostrating myself again and again.*

So with respect to the actual act of confession, we recall the negative actions we have committed. We then bring the understanding of these actions will result in negative defects to mind. We see that when these actions were committed, they were committed out of ignorance, not knowing the result to come. We have accumulated negative karma through body, speech and mind. Recalling this, and understanding the ensuing results, we humbly prostrate to all buddhas and bodhisattvas. We visualize that all buddhas and bodhisattvas are seated in front of us, and in their presence we then confess all evil actions.

The last verse of this section is related to the fourth power, which is concerned with resolving not to commit any negative actions again. The verse is as follows:

65. *May the Leaders accept my sin and transgression! That which was not good, Lords, will not be done again by me.*

So we confess negative actions that have accumulated and resolve not to do them again. If we confess without having resolved not to commit such actions again, then we haven't really regretted the negative actions that we committed. It is necessary to understand that we have acted incorrectly and also important to then vow not to commit such actions again. If confession is done in this way, we are able to purify the negative actions committed.

The type of confession that has been explained is related to karma, cause and effect. If we accumulate unvirtue, the result will be suffering. If we accumulate virtue, the result will be happiness. Since unvirtue results in suffering, it is necessary to know how to go about confession. The *law of karma* was taught by the Buddha. The Buddha taught that the cause and effect aspect of karma is quite difficult to comprehend or understand. For example, in Ethiopia where for there has been for many years a great famine. So those that take rebirth in such a country then obviously will have to experience hunger and famine. The cause for them taking rebirth in such a place is their former accumulated karma. There is no other reason for them taking birth in such an unpleasant place. So we can see that there is no one but oneself that is responsible for the conditions under which one is reborn. Then there are those that are born, for example, in America or Europe. They have no difficulties generally speaking with respect to food and so forth and do not have the same difficulties as those that have been born in, for example, Ethiopia. We may wonder, "Who sends, so to speak, these people to places such as American and Europe?" In fact, they weren't sent there by anyone. The reason for them taking birth in these countries is their own karma. If we accumulate negative karma, difficulties will ensue. If we accumulate good karma, happiness will ensue.

So the law of karma is whatever we experience has been created by ourselves. If we experience suffering, we have totally brought about this ourselves. If we experience happiness, we have also brought about that condition. There are those that think that once they've committed negative actions, they cannot change the course of events. However, with the methods for confessing negative actions we can purify or eliminate future suffering that is the result of our negative actions. So in fact we has the possibility to change the course of events by means of practicing virtue and so forth.

Questions

Question: How does one offer one's body?
Rinpoche: Generally we cherish our body more than anything else that exists in the world. We then offer our body to counteract the attachment that we have for our body. When making the offering, we just think of our body as it is and offer it. There is no need to mentally create a very vivid image of it or that we have to offer an extremely beautiful body; we just offer out body however it is. Having offered our body, we should

realize that we are to accomplish the wishes and desires of the three and rare supreme ones. That is to say, that from that point onwards, we will apply ourselves to the practice of virtue and give up non-virtue. We will do however much we are able to do with respect of helping the benefit of beings, since this is what pleases the three rare and supreme ones.

Question: Do persons who are nonBuddhists or have not taken the bodhisattva vows possess awakening mind or bodhichitta?

Rinpoche: There are fortunate beings in the world who have many good intentions and these one could say have bodhichitta: But the majority of those that are endowed with bodhichitta are to be found within the Buddhist tradition because Buddhists have an understanding of bodhichitta and know it's meaning. Bodhichitta generally means that one has developed goodness of mind or one has good intentions. But these good intentions might be limited to having good intentions in relation to relatives, one's country, one's race, and so forth. If one, for example, has good intentions towards one's relatives, it follows that one might be adverse to those that are not one's relatives. If one has good intentions in relations to one's country, it follows one will probably have bad intentions towards other countries. Similarly, having good intentions towards those that are of the same race means one is probably adverse towards others of a different race. With bodhichitta, however, one is not biased and one's good intentions includes all sentient beings. One believes that all sentient beings no matter what country they belong to, whether they are related or not, or whether they belong to the race or not, desire happiness and want to avoid suffering. So a bodhisattva's good intentions include all these sentient beings and is completely unbiased.

There are many people that have good intentions and desire to help others, but their good intentions are limited. They think that it's not necessary to attain Buddhahood and it is sufficient to be happy oneself and benefit others so that they are happy. In actual fact, one needs to establish all beings in Buddhahood because any other help is only temporary and will eventually be exhausted. For example, if one lends a hundred dollars to someone, for some time that person will have money and be temporarily helped, but when the money is used up, that person is impoverished as before. Whereas if one is able to establish someone in Buddhahood, that is the ultimate kind of help and will never be exhausted.

Question: You mentioned that in Nepal and India there are many holy places where we can prostrate and the merit accumulated from these places is immeasurable. But most of the time we are not able to visit these places.

Rinpoche: The merit is the same whether we actually are at the place or not. The point of being in such sacred places is that we see this is a very holy place in front of us and this fact is very helpful in engendering faith and devotion in us. But if we visualize prostrating in such a place, the ensuing merit is the same. In other words, we don't have to be àt the actual location.

Question: Can you explain what it means for the buddhas to accept one's evil and wrongs?

Rinpoche: One could express that in a different way. This line means that one confesses to the buddhas and bodhisattvas seated in front of one. One then realizes and understands that one has acted in a mistaken way. One also knows that the buddhas and bodhisattvas know of one's mistaken ways, and one, so to speak, asks all buddhas and bodhisattvas to "accept one's evil and wrongs." This means that in fact, when one committed these evil actions, one didn't have a correct understanding of what one was doing. One then tells this to the buddhas and bodhisattvas in front of one and asks them to accept the negative actions one has committed. Then having confessed in such a way that one committed these evil actions out of ignorance, they will then show the path or method by means of which one is able to counteract whatever was committed. So it is for that reason one asks them to accept one's evil and wrongs, asks them to have the knowledge of one's evils and wrongs so that they may teach one or show one the path, or the unmistaken path by means of which these evil actions are counteracted or cleared away.

Question: What is the actual confession practice?

Rinpoche: One actually recites the actual lines 54 to 62 of Shantideva and then one identifies unwholesomeness or evil actions. Then one recites verse 64:

64. I confess it all, standing in the presence of the Lords, fearing sorrow, and with folded hands prostrating myself again and again.

and one actually meditates on the object of confession, which is applying oneself to remedial force. One has at this point developed some fear of the misery that one is to experience. In order to counteract that, with folded hands one prostrates oneself again and again, makes offerings to the buddhas and bodhisattvas in front of the one that one has meditated on, and so forth. So in that verse, the actual practice or practices by means of which one accumulates virtue are performed.

Question: I want to ask a practical question. If you do an evil deed during the day, should you try to confess it right away, or should you

wait until the end of the day or should you wait until you practice?
Rinpoche: It doesn't make a big difference when one confesses evil deeds. One confesses what one has done the moment one recognizes that one has committed an evil deed. Whether a day has elapsed, whether it's immediately or after a few years makes no great difference. At the point when one recognizes that one has committed an evil deed and regrets that, one makes a confession. With respect to commitment of the *Vajrayana* tradition on the other hand, timeliness have been mentioned, though generally speaking with respect to evil actions there are no particular time limits.

Question: Does one have to feel remorse with confession?
Rinpoche: Here confession is concerned with recognizing or identifying evil deeds that one has committed. It's not very important to have a feeling of remorse or regret for no particular reason. With respect to confession or disclosure of evil, one actually recalls negative deeds and regrets them.

Question: What about regret?
Rinpoche: Well, usually with regret, one has a reason. There is something one has done in a mistaken way and one recognizes this. And therefore one feels remorse or regret. Though generally speaking, the nature of samsara is suffering and so forth. So when this state of mind arises without any particular reason, it's good to meditate or do some practice which could clear away that frame of mind. It just indicates the general nature of samsara and suffering, the fact that state of mind arises.

Question: Is it important to visualize the buddhas and bodhisattvas?
Rinpoche: Well, buddhas and bodhisattvas are not ordinary beings. There is the interaction between oneself meditating on the buddhas and bodhisattvas and the buddhas and bodhisattvas knowing that one is doing this act of confession. So we are not able to actually see these buddhas and bodhisattvas in front of us, but they are present. We evoke them then by doing this meditation and not being ordinary beings, they at that point know that we are doing this confession, and they actually are present in front of us.

Question: How far away should one visualize them?
Rinpoche: There is no ordinary distance. For them, it's not a question of being far away or close by. They are not present in front of us physically. They are present in the sense that they are aware of our confession.

Question: Could you explain the fourth power a little more.
Rinpoche: The fourth power is very much related to the first which is remorse or regret for evil actions committed. If one hasn't developed the

first power thoroughly, the fourth won't purify negative deeds whereas if one concentrates on the first power and develops it thoroughly, then the fourth power will come along all by itself.

We are able to purify or clear away the effects from these non-virtues, but that actual attitude has to be changed through the practice of meditation. So it is a question of eliminating effects coming from these states of mind, but the actual state of mind must be changed by means of the practice of meditation.

The first power is to identify and recognize negative deeds. If one has a thorough understanding of the many faults that ensue from wrong deeds, then naturally one will avoid them. So not being able to give up wrong views originates with not having a thorough understanding of faults and defects that ensue from wrong views.

The Seven Branch Practice
(Tib. yan lag bdun pa)

Almost all Deity practices incorporate the seven branch practice within them usually at the beginning. These are given in A Guide to the Bodhisattva's Way of Life. They are:

1. Supplicating the Buddhas and Bodhisattvas by prostrating to the three jewels (the Buddha who created the Buddhist teachings, the dharma which are the Buddhist teachings and the sangha who are the practitioners on the path who help us understand the Buddhist teachings).
2. The making of offerings which are associated with body, speech, and mind. Body or material offerings are things such as flowers, scented water, and food. Verbal offerings are reciting songs of praise for the Buddhas and Bodhisattvas. Mental offerings are often offering all the accumulated merit one has acquired.
3. Confessing negative actions and thus purifying unvirtuous habits. One admits to doing the negative deed, one feels true remorse and then one resolves not to do it again.
4. Rejoicing in the virtue of others. This strengthens one resolve to do only positive actions and also it helps overcome jealousy that one might have when others do things we haven't done.
5. Requesting the Buddhas to teach by turning the wheel of dharma.
6. Asking the Buddhas not to pass into nirvana, but to keep coming back to earth to help more sentient beings.
7. Dedicating the merit of everything positive that one does for the benefit of others, and not for the benefit of oneself, which is the true bodhisattva way and a way to develop bodhichitta.

Chapter 3

The Full Acceptance of
the Awakening Mind

In the Buddha's tradition, all phenomena are considered to come into existence through two ways: the principle cause and through the *secondary conditions*. The principle cause is the actual cause. The secondary conditions aid the development of the particular phenomenon to come into existence. If one considers a flower, one starts out sowing the seed in the ground. The seed is then the principle cause and water, manure, warmth and so forth that contributes to the growing of the seed into a flower are the secondary causes. Without these secondary conditions the flower couldn't come into existence. So these secondary conditions aid in the manifestation of something. These two causes exist in respect to all phenomena.

What are the principle cause and secondary conditions for bodhichitta or awakening mind? The second chapter of the text four of the eight branches of offering are covered, these being making offerings, paying homage, taking refuge, and confession. In the third chapter of the text, one finds the four latter offerings being discussed: to rejoice in virtue, to request the wheel of the dharma to be turned, to request those that have attained enlightenment not to pass into nirvana but to remain in the world, and finally dedication and aspiration of bodhichitta. These eight branches correspond to secondary conditions which aid the development of the awakening mind and are dependent upon the accumulation of merit. The principle cause for the arousing of awakening mind is to purify one's mind, by training in various practices, and to achieve the welfare of all beings. We will not discuss the third factor which is full acceptance of the awakening mind.

Rejoicing in Virtue

The branch of rejoicing in virtue is taught in the first four verses:

1. I rejoice in exultation at the goodness, and at the cessation and destruction of sorrow, wrought by all beings. May those who sorrow achieve joy!

2. I rejoice at the release of embodied beings from the sorrowful wheel of rebirth.

3. I rejoice at the Bodhisattvahood and at the Buddhahood of those who have attained salvation.

4. I rejoice at the Oceans of Determination, the Bearers of Happiness to all beings, the Vehicles of Advantage for all beings, and those who teach.[9]

5. With folded hands, I beseech the perfect Buddhas in all places: May they cause the light of the Dharma to shine upon those who, because of confusion, have fallen into sorrow.

Individuals usually become jealous of those who are able to accomplish what they desire, or people that do something that is a good accomplishment. The antidote for such jealousy is to rejoice or take joy in the good deeds done by others. On seeing somebody doing something good and achieving good results, we should rejoice rather than being jealous. We should think that this person is very good and has done something good. To rejoice is an outstanding method for the accumulation of merit.

Rejoicing in the Accumulation of Merit

The way in which we meditate when rejoicing in the virtue accumulated by others has three types of objects of one's practice or meditation: The virtue accumulated by an individual of inferior capacity, the virtue accumulated by an individual of average capacity, and the virtue accumulated by an individual of superior capacity. With each of these three there are two aspects: cause and effect. The cause is then the accumulation of merit and the effect is experiencing the pleasant result of that. So there are three aspects with respect to the focus of meditation, when meditating on rejoicing in the virtue of others.

The virtues inferior individuals accumulated is slight and their motivation is inferior. The result of the virtue they accumulate is that they avoid taking rebirth in any of the *three lower realms*.[10] They take instead rebirth in any of the *three higher realms*: the god, the jealous god, or the human realm. So temporarily, they do not have to experience any suffering. This type condition is like being able to have a rest, one temporarily doesn't have to experience any suffering. Even though it's only a temporary relief from samsara, we should rejoice in that virtue thinking it's very fortunate for these individuals to be able to live in happy circumstances at least for some time. And thinking in this way, we should rejoice in the virtue they have accumulated.

We rejoice in the cause which is the actual accumulation of merit. The effect is that one is free from the suffering of the lower realms because of the virtue accumulated. Someone with this inferior capacity who has accumulated this merit would, for example, will take rebirth as a human being and would therefore not have to experience any suffering, living in fortunate circumstances. So the effect of this virtue accumulated is temporary happiness and we should then take joy thinking that they are very fortunate.

The virtue accumulated by those of medium or average capacity relates to the *shravakas* and *pratyekabuddhas*. The happiness they experience resulting from their practice of virtue is that they are forever freed from the suffering of samsara and they experience happiness which continues. We should then rejoice in both aspects of cause and effect. The cause is their practice of virtue is the accumulation of merit. The effect is that they become free from samsara and do not have to again experience suffering in this conditioned existence. So we should think of these beings as very fortunate and rejoice in their virtue.

Those of superior capacity are very courageous having no concern of self, but instead have unbiased concern for all sentient beings as vast as space. We rejoice in the effect of the virtue practiced of these beings. The effect has two aspects: the ultimate attainment of Buddhahood on a temporary level and the attainment of the bodhisattva levels on the absolute level. One continues to rejoice in the cause of that effect, which again has two aspects. The cause which is the practice of virtue and their motivation which is very vast lasting an extremely long period of time. In fact these beings practice virtue for the sake of all sentient beings and have resolved to do so until all beings have been freed from samsara. They have resolved to be diligent by working with joyous effort until samsara has been emptied. Therefore their motivation is very vast like an ocean. This motivation is not just something which they bring to mind and do not put into practice. There is this motivation and the actual activity by means of which these beings accomplish the welfare of others.

Turning the Wheel of Dharma

The seventh branch is to request the wheel of the dharma to be turned. That is taught in the fifth verse:

6. With folded hands, I beseech the Conquerors who are desirous of experiencing cessation: May they pause for countless eons lest this world become blind.

The historical Buddha, the *Buddha Shakyamuni*, attained enlightenment at Bodh Gaya after which he didn't teach the dharma for seven days. There were two reasons for not teaching immediately. One was to enable beings to understand that the dharma, the teachings, are very rare. The reason for not teaching immediately was to enable beings to develop appreciation of the teachings. If teachings are given easily, such appreciation may not arise. The second reason was to enable those that request the teachings to accumulate vast virtue. By requesting teaching, one accumulates great merit. The historical Buddha after attaining enlightenment thought to himself, "What I have realized? The dharma that I have realized is profound and peaceful. It is so profound and peaceful that in fact other beings won't be able to comprehend it." So he decided to meditate in solitude, thinking that beings would not be able to understand these teachings. At that point, two gods, Bhrama and Indra, requested him to turn the wheel of the dharma, and because of that request, the Buddha started to teach.

So the historical Buddha is an example of turning the wheel of dharma. There are many other universes in which many buddhas reside. Some of these buddhas do not teach. We then request all buddhas to teach for the reason that all beings have fallen into a state of suffering. Out of ignorance, they do not know how to avoid suffering and achieve happiness which they desire, so in order to enable beings to accomplish happiness which they desire, we request all the buddhas to teach the dharma so that all beings may come to experience happiness.

The next verse is concerned with requesting these beings not to pass into nirvana. There are enlightened beings that consider their work to be finished and therefore, they decide to pass into nirvana. One then requests these beings not to pass into nirvana, since it would result in that people would become like blind people having no one to guide them. We therefore requests these beings to remain for a very long period of time and teach. The next set of verses are concerned with the eighth branch of offering which is dedication and aspiration:

7. Having done all this, let me also be a cause of abatement, by means of whatever good I have achieved, for all of the sorrow of all creatures.

8. I am medicine for the sick. May I be their physician and their servant, until sickness does not arise again.

9. With rains of food and drink may I dispel the anguish of hunger and thirst. In the famine of the intermediary eons between the world cycles (antarakalpa) may I be food and drink;

10. May I be an imperishable treasury for needy beings. May I stand in their presence in order to do what is beneficial in every possible way.

There are two aspects with respect to aspiration and praise. One may be able to accomplish these and one may not be able to accomplish these. For example, if one prays very strongly for that a flower will grow out of a table. This will never happen. It's not possible to make that happen no matter how strongly one may pray for it. Having developed the inclination to have a flower grow, one then will make an effort towards accomplishing it. So the initial inclination in itself is not sufficient because effort is also needed. One will need to find a pot, fill it with earth, plant the seed and so forth. So the initial inclination then results in that what one prayed for will become accomplished through one's personal effort. So the source of our prayers coming true or being accomplished is the effort. With respect to awakening mind, there is the initial desire to relieve beings of suffering such as famine. So that's the first motivation or inclination one has. Then depending upon the effort we take towards this end, we gradually achieve what we have prayed for.

So in Verse 11 we make a vow to achieve the principal cause which is for the sake of others:

11. I sacrifice indifferently my bodies, pleasures, and goodness, where the three ways cross [past, present, and future], for the complete fulfillment of the welfare of all beings.

The next verse then gives the reason for why we need to give up everything for the sake of others:

12. The abandonment of all is Nirvana, and my mind (manas) seeks Nirvana. If all is to be sacrificed by me, it is best that it be given to beings.

This verse then says why we should give up everything such as our body, virtue and so forth for the sake of others. If we do that when alive that giving up will remedy the belief in self, ego clinging, and ultimately result in Buddhahood which we need to attain. If we don't give up everything when alive, we will have to give up everything anyway, such as our body, possessions and so forth at death. That is to say, at the time of death, we have to leave everything behind. If everything is given up in that way, namely that we just leave everything behind at death having held onto it during life, then the effect will no great benefit, whereas if we, on the other hand, give up or is able to give up everything when alive, then the benefit will be very great. The verse then says that we might as well give it up while alive since at death everything has to be left behind.

12. *I deliver this body to the pleasure of all creatures. May they strike! May they revile! May they cover it constantly with refuse!*
13. *May they play with my body! May they laugh! And may they be amused! I have given my body to them. What do I care about its misfortune?*

The two verses above are related to giving away our body to all sentient beings. The next set of verses are concerned with aspirations or prayers.[11] One prays for being able to give beings whatever they desire, being able to benefit them and fulfill all their desires.

15. *May they do whatever deeds bring pleasure to them, but let there never be any misfortune because of having relied on me.*
16. *If their opinion regarding me should be either irritable or pleasant, let it nonetheless be their perpetual means to the complete fulfillment of every aim.*
17. *Those who wrong me, and those who accuse me falsely, and those who mock, and others: May they all be sharers in Enlightenment.*
18. *I would be a protector for those without protection, a leader for those who journey, and a boat, a bridge, a passage for those desiring the further shore.*
19. *For all creatures, I would be a lantern for those desiring a lantern, I would be a bed for those desiring a bed, I would be a slave for those desiring a slave.*
20. *I would be for creatures a magic jewel, an inexhaustible jar, a powerful spell, an universal remedy, a wishing tree, and a cow of plenty.*
21. *As the earth and other elements are, in various ways, for the enjoyment of innumerable beings dwelling in all of space;*
22. *So may I be, in various ways, the means of sustenance for the living beings occupying space, for as long a time as all are not satisfied.*

These verses are concerned with the way in which awakening mind or bodhichitta is aroused. Generally speaking, the mind of humans are not very stable. We therefore need to resolve to do something. A person may one day, for example, say, "Well, I won't take this and that as the truth today, and I want this and that," anything that he or she perceives of as good or desirous. The next day, the very same person might not believe that anymore. Our mind changes a lot. We have many different likes and dislikes, and they are not very stable. With this instability, it is difficult to accomplish. Some people upon hearing about awakening mind think that it is very important. They think, "I must develop this." and so forth. Later, however, they may think, "I can't really do it. It's too difficult." Because of changing mind, the effect of having aroused bodhichitta is very slight. Therefore, we must strongly resolve to arouse bodhichitta. We should resolve to do so no matter what type of difficulties one encounters and to engender it for a very, very long period of time in a very vast way.

In contrast, the vows of individual liberation (Skt. *pratimoksha*) are related to physical and verbal activity and are extremely difficult to restore once they have been broken, though they are easy to keep. If we decide not to steal, we just stay away from stealing. It's not difficult. And if we decide not to take the lives of any beings, we just stay away from doing so. It's not very difficult. When these vows have been broken, then they have been compared to a broken clay pot. Once a clay pot has been broken, it is difficult to repair. On the other hand, bodhisattva vows are said to be like a golden vase. Even though we might drop it and dent it, we can repair it. So these vows are easy to break, but also easy to restore partly because the bodhisattva vows are related to mental activity. Many thoughts arise in our mind. Some accord with the bodhisattva way of life and do not. We can then easily change our frame of mind. Therefore there is no great fault even though we may have mentally broken our bodhisattva vows, since by changing our frame of mind they are restored. Therefore these vows are said to be like a golden vase, easy to repair or restore.

The Resolve to Raise Bodhichitta

The two following verses are the actual taking of the bodhisattva vow. The words of Shantideva have actually been borrowed for the actual *bodhisattva vow* ceremony and *ngondro* practice[12] and are as follows:

23. *As the ancient Buddhas seized the Awakening Mind, and in like manner they followed regularly on the path of Bodhisattva instruction;*
24. *Thus also do I cause the Awakening mind to arise for the welfare of the world, and thus shall I practice these instructions in proper order.*

So not only did the bodhisattvas of old give rise to bodhichitta, they also progressively dwelt in the bodhisattva practices for the sake of all beings. And in the same way or fashion, we resolve to engender bodhichitta and follow the associated practices. These two verses are concerned with resolving to give rise to bodhichitta. The actual giving of the promise to engender the awakening mind is in itself not sufficient. Once we have resolved to engender bodhichitta, it must be increased. The best method for increasing bodhichitta is then to take joy in any associated activity. Generally speaking, if we do something and is satisfied with it, then naturally the associated activity will expand and flourish. If one on the other hand does something and afterwards thinks, "Well, this wasn't really the thing to do. It wasn't very good," then any associated activity will decrease. For that reason, we should, once we have resolved to engender bodhichitta, take joy in any associated activity to make it increase. We start out then to take joy in the engendered of bodhichitta in ourselves.

25. *The wise man, having considered serenely the Awakening mind, should rejoice, for the sake of its growth and its well-being, in the thought:*
26. *Today my birth is completed, my human nature is most appropriate; today I have been born into the Buddha-family and I am now a Buddha-son.*
27. *It is now for me to behave according to the customary behavior of one's own family, in order that there may be no stain put upon that spotless family.*
28. *As a blind man may obtain a jewel in a heap of dust, so, somehow, this awakening mind has arisen even within me.*
29. *This elixir has originated for the destruction of death in the world. It is the imperishable treasure which alleviates the world's poverty.*
30. *It is the uttermost medicine, the abatement of the world's disease. It is a tree of rest for the wearied world journeying on the road of being.*
31. *When crossing over hard places, it is the universal bridge for all travelers. It is the risen moon of mind, the soothing of the world's disturbing emotions).*
32. *It is a great sun dispelling the darkness of the world's ignorance. It is fresh butter, surging up from the churning of the milk of the true Dharma.*
33. *For the caravan of humanity, moving along the road of being, hungering for the enjoyment of happiness, this happiness banquet is prepared for the complete refreshening of every being who comes to it.*

The awakening mind of bodhichitta is said to be the supreme nectar which overcomes death. It is said to be the inexhaustible treasure that dispels all poverty. It's said to be the supreme medicine that quells all disease.

Generally speaking, there is no method to eliminate death. However, if we develop bodhichitta, we will ultimately attain Buddhahood, which means we have attained a state of selflessness. Therefore bodhichitta is said to be the nectar which overcomes death. Similarly, if we attain Buddhahood, we will have freed ourselves from all disease, so bodhichitta is said to be the supreme of all medicines. Similarly, it's said to be like a inexhaustible treasure dispelling the poverty of the world since once we have attained Buddhahood, we will not experience poverty anymore.

The last verse of this chapter is related to exhorting others to rejoice in what we have done, mainly taking the vows of a bodhisattva. So the verses up to here were concerned with ourselves rejoicing in what we have just done. Now the following verse is concerned with exhorting others to rejoice in this. So the verse is as follows:

33. Now I invite the world to Buddhahood, and, incidentally, to happiness. May gods, anti-gods (asuras), and others, truly rejoice in the presence of all the Protectors.

So we ask everyone to be joyful since at this point we have promised to help others and free them from suffering. We have resolved to do so, in the presence in all the bodhisattvas. Therefore in the future, we will be able to relieve others of their suffering. It is for this reason, we ask them to take joy in what one has just done.

Questions

Question: I do not understand what was meant by there being many different universes?
Rinpoche: In the Buddhist tradition, it is taught that there are many other universes in which there are other buddhas, other enlightened beings. Some of them teach the dharma, some of them don't, and the text, is concerned that we request these buddhas that do not teach the dharma, to do so.

Chapter 4

Conscientiousness

[Thrangu Rinpoche did not have time to cover this chapter so we include the root verses only.]

1. *The son of the Conqueror, having grasped the Thought of Enlightenment firmly, must make every effort, constantly and alertly, not to transgress the discipline (siksa).*
2. *Whatever is undertaken in haste, whatever is not properly considered, may be accomplished or it may not be accomplished, even if a vow has been taken;*
3. *but that which has been considered by the Buddhas, who have great wisdom (prajna) and by their sons; and even by me, according to my ability how can that be neglected?*
4. *And if, having thus promised, I do not fulfill my vow in deed, having falsely said all of this, what will be my destiny?*
5. *The man who, having mentally reflected, will not give again [and again], will become a hungry ghost, so it has been said, even if the matter is trifling.*
6. *How much more the being who loudly has proclaimed the supreme happiness! Having spoken falsely to all the world, what will be my destiny?*
7. *Only the All-knowing One understands the inscrutable course of action which releases those men even after the Thought of Enlightenment has been forsaken.*
8. *Every transgression of the Bodhisattva is of extreme gravity, since, as he transgresses, the welfare of all beings is destroyed because of it.*
9. *Anyone who creates an obstacle to his merit, even for an instant, has no limit to his misfortune; because he destroys the welfare of others.*
10. *Indeed, the one who has smitten the benefactor of even a single being, will be smitten. How much more when he smites the beings who dwell throughout the immensity of all space?*
11. *As a consequence he is buffeted in the cycle of rebirth between the power of transgression and the power of the Thought of Enlightenment; he delays a long while the obtaining of the*

bodhisattva stages.

12. Therefore, that which has been promised, is to be zealously fulfilled by me. If today an effort is not made, I sink lower and lower.

13 Innumerable Buddhas have passed, seeking all beings: Because of my own fault I have been beyond the scope of their medicine.

14 If even today I am to be as I have been time after time, I really deserve to receive misfortune, disease, death, mutilation, laceration, and so forth.

15. When shall I obtain the arising of a Buddha, faith, humanity, and a condition suitable for the practice of righteous actions? These are requirements very hard to obtain!

16 This day of health and its nourishment, the lack of danger and this momentary life, like a borrowed body, are a deception.

17 Surely, because of such actions as mine, the human state will not be achieved again. In failure to achieve the human state, there is evil: from whence can good come?

18. If I do not do good when I am capable of goodness, what will I do when I am stupefied by the sorrows of an evil destiny?

19. Because of the lack of good actions and, indeed, the accumulation of evil, the very idea of an advantageous condition of life is destroyed for hundreds of millions of eons.

20. Therefore the Blessed One said that the human state is exceedingly hard to obtain; it is like a turtle inserting his neck into the cleft of a yoke in the great sea.

21. Because of the evil wrought in a single instant, one is placed in the Avici hell for an eon. Because of the evil accumulated in an eternity of time, a good state is out of the question.

22. Even after having experienced that duration [of sorrow], one is not released, because while it is being experienced other evil is begotten.

23. Having obtained a brief moment which is endowed with such qualities, there is certainly no greater deception and no greater stupidity than not applying myself to goodness;

24. and if, indeed, I am again distressed and I sit stupidly inactive, once more I shall burn for a long while as I am driven on by the messengers of death.

25. Long will my body bum in the intolerable fires of hell. Long will my unruly mind burn in the flame of remorse.

26. How, indeed, has this propitious state, so hard to obtain, ever been achieved? And am I to be knowingly led again into those very hells?

27. Like one who is stupefied by mantras, I have no understanding of this, not realizing by whom I am crazed or who stands there within me.

28. *My enemies desire, hatred, and such like are destitute of hands, feet, and so forth. They are not courageous, and they are not wise. How can I be enslaved by them?*

28. *Yet they are dwelling within my own mind, and thus they smite me at their ease. Nonetheless, I am not angry. Pitiful is this unseasonable patience!*

30 *If all gods and men were my enemies, they would not be capable of pulling me into the fire of the Avici hell,*

31.*at whose mere touch even ashes may not remain of Mount Meru; [but] my powerful disturbing emotions, my enemies, instantly cast me there.*

32. *None, of all other enemies, is endowed with the long life, without beginning or end, which is the great length of life of my enemies of disturbing emotions.*

33. *All may be turned to advantage when service is done because of kindness; but these disturbing emotions, being served, become even more the creators of sorrow.*

34 *When these constant and long-lived enemies, the only causes begetting a flood of misfortune, dwell within the heart; how can I, without fear, find pleasure on the wheel of rebirth?*

35. *If these guards of the prison of being, the executioners of those to be slain in hell and elsewhere, stand in the house of the mind, in the cage of greed; how can I be happy?*

36 *Indeed, I will not be free from their torment until these enemies are slain before my eyes. Proud men, when concerned with even a very slight offender, are dominated by anger, and they will not sleep until the enemy has been destroyed.*

37 *The strong are able to ignore in violent battle the aforementioned death, suffering, and ignorance. The incalculable suffering of wounds caused by arrows and spears does not bring about such aversion as those enemies who are still to be overcome.*

38. *How then can there be despondency and depression, when I have begun to strike these natural enemies, the continual causes of all sorrow? In spite of hundreds of misfortunes, what could be the excuse?*

39. *Others bear the wounds of enemies, although they are useless, like ornaments upon their bodies. So why should I, who am engaged in the accomplishment of the Great Work (maharthasiddhi) be oppressed by sorrows?*

40. *Their minds fixed upon the means of livelihood, fishermen, outcastes*

(candalas), farmers, and the like, prevail over the misfortunes of cold, heat, and similar difficulties. How shall I not prevail in the work of the world's well-being?

41. *When I promised the world, extending as far as the ten points of space, liberation from the disturbing emotions, I was myself not liberated from them.*

42. *Having been ignorant of my own measure, a madman then spoke. To the extent that I am not turned around, I will always be bound by passion.*

43. *I will be a fighter in this, and an enemy intent upon waging war, except with regard to that kind of disturbing emotions which results from the destruction of disturbing emotions.*

44. *Although my bowels ooze out and my head falls, I will not bow before my everlasting enemies, the passions.*

45 *An enemy who has been banished may find rest in another quarter and then return With accumulated power; but the enemy of passion has not such a destiny.*

46. *Where will he go who dwells in my mind, when once cast out? Where will he stand from which he may strive after my destruction? I am stupid only because I make no effort. It is by the perception of wisdom (prajna) that the vile passions are to be subdued.*

47 *The passions are not in objects, nor in the complex of the senses, nor in any intermediate place, nor elsewhere. Where are they, these that torture the whole world! They are simply illusion (maya). 0 heart, renounce fear! Strive for wisdom (prajna) Why do you torture yourselves in hell without cause?*

48. *Having deliberated in this way, I shall strive for the behavior taught in the discipline. How is he healed, who, needing to be treated with medicine, departs from the prescription of the physician?*

Chapter 5

Guarding Alertness

[Rinpoche did not discuss this chapter so we include the root verses and a commentary on mindfulness and alertness which comes from his *Looking Directly at Mind: The Moonlight of Mahamudra*]

1. *In order to observe a rule of life (siksa) the mind must zealously be guarded. It is not possible to observe any discipline without guarding the quivering mind.*
2. *Unsubdued and overwrought elephants do not effect that damage here which the unrestrained mind, an elephant roaming wild, does in the Avici hell and elsewhere.*
3. *If this elephant of mind is bound on all sides by the cord of mindfulness (smrti), all fear disappears and complete happiness comes.*
4. *All enemies: tigers, lions, elephants, bears, serpents; and all the keepers of hell: the demons and the horrors (raksasas)*
5. *all of these are bound by the mastery of one's mind; and by the subduing of that one mind, all are subdued:*
6. *because from the mind are derived all fears and immeasurable sorrows. Thus it was taught by the Speaker of Truth.*
7. *By whom were the swords in hell carefully prepared? By whom the hot iron pavement? And whence were born its women?*
8. *All that, taught the Sage, was produced by the evil mind. Therefore, nothing except that which is derived from mind is fearsome in the three worlds.*
9 *If the perfection of charity (dana) could have made the world without poverty, it must not have been an attribute of the ancient Saviors, since even today the world is poor!*
10. *Yet by the mere thought of forsaking all of our possessions for the sake of all creatures, along with the [consequent] merit [of this great act], the perfection of charity is proclaimed. It is thus only mind.*
11. *Where can fish and others be led, from whence I may not destroy them? But when the thought of cessation is obtained, that is regarded as the perfection of conduct (silaparamita).*

12. *How many enemies, measureless as the sky, will I be able to destroy? Yet when the thought of anger is destroyed, all enemies are destroyed.*
13. *Where is the leather which will be able to cover all of the earth? The earth is covered by the amount of leather in a sandal.*
14. *In the same way, I am not at all able to restrain exterior powers, but if I will restrain my own mind, what matters a lack of restraint by others?*
15. *There is no merit derived from sluggish conduct in speech and body, but the nobility of the Brahman resides in the industrious and the single-minded.*
16. *If the sluggish mind is fixed on something else, all prayers and austerities are useless, even if practiced for a long time. Thus taught the All-knowing One.*
17. *To destroy sorrow, to obtain joy, [creatures of a sluggish mind] wander in vain through space; for by such [creatures] this mysterious mind, the embodiment of all Dharma, is not understood.*
18. *Hence the mind is to be well regulated and well protected by me. Neglecting the vow of mind protection (cittaraksa), what is the use to me of frequent vows?*
19. *As one standing in the midst of a crowd carefully protects a wound, so one standing in the midst of evil persons always should protect the mind as an open wound.*
20. *Afraid of experiencing pain in a wound, I carefully protect that wound. Afraid of being caught between the crushing mountains of hell, why should I not protect the mind as if it were a wound?*
21. *What of an ascetic living a blameless way of life, even among rogues or even in the midst of wanton women? He does not interrupt his constancy.*
22. *Let my possessions be lost love, respect, the life of the body. Let any other happiness be lost to me, but never [mastery of] the mind.*
23. *For those desiring to protect the mind, I fold my hands in prayer: With all zeal protect both mindfulness) and total awareness (samprajanya).*
24. *As a man troubled by disease is not capable of any action, so likewise with regard to these virtues [smirti and samprajanya], the troubled mind is incapable of any action.*
25. *When practiced by the mind without total awareness, instruction and reflection escape from mindfulness like water from a leaking jar.*
26. *Many who have been instructed, who are faithful and intent upon zeal, become sinful and impure because of a lack of awareness.*

27. *Because of that thief, lack of awareness, who pursues the theft of mindfulness, those whose accumulated merits have been stolen, come to an evil state.*

28. *The disturbing emotions, a monastic brotherhood (sangha) of thieves, seek this incarnation (avatara). Having seized this incarnation they rob and they destroy one's happy state of life.*

29 *Therefore, mindfulness never should be with drawn from the gateway of the mind, but once gone, it should be restored by full recollection of the pain of hell.*

30. *For those fortunate ones who exert themselves even out of fear of being punished by a teacher mindfulness is easily generated by living with a guru.*

31. *The Buddhas and the Bodhisattvas are everywhere, unimpeded, and instantaneous. All is in their presence. I am standing before them.*

32. *After meditating on these matters, one should be filled with shame, with reverence, with fear. Remembrance of the Buddha should return to one again and again.*

33. *Total awareness then comes and does not escape again, when mindfulness stands at the gateway of the mind for the sake of its protection.*

34. *Primarily, then, such a thought as this is always to be fostered: I should ever remain passive as a piece of wood.*

35. *The eyes never should be directed to and fro without purpose. The vision constantly should be directed down wards as in meditation.*

36. *But for the purpose of resting the vision, one sometimes may look to the distance, and having seen that which is mere appearance, he may look at it for the sake of greeting.*

37. *On the road and elsewhere one sometimes may look to the four quarters in apprehension. Having rested and having turned around, he may look to the region behind.*

38. *After observing that one may proceed forwards, or that one may proceed backwards, having been thus enlightened, one ought to perform his duty in all circumstances.*

39. *Moreover, after the body has been properly placed, one should resolve to keep it in a particular position. How that body ought to be placed should frequently be reexamined again and again.*

40. *The mad elephant of the mind must be watched zealously in order that his bonds be not released from that great pillar of reflection which is the Dharma.*

41. As the mind should be examined with the thought, "Where does it wander?" so one should not cast off the yoke of contemplation even for an instant.

42. Although one is powerless to act for the best when bound by fear, agitation, and so forth, still, on an occasion of charity, the overlooking of conventional morality (sila) is advised.

43. Whoever, having been enlightened, commences to act, ought to think of nothing else. Insofar as this can be accomplished it is by means of applying one's entire being.

44. This way, everything is well done. Otherwise, both [of the conflicting interests of charity and morality] may not be achieved. And the flaw of nonawareness (asamprajanya) will attain further development.

45. My desire is gone, because of destroying manifold chatterings, frequent turnings, all curiosities.

46. One ought to reject useless scratching, fidgeting, puttering, once having learned the discipline of the Tathagatha and having feared it.

47. If one should desire to move, or desire to speak, his mind is to be examined and suitably composed with patience.

48. If one would see his mind disciplined and blunted, then he should not act nor speak. He should remain like a piece of wood.

49. If the mind should be arrogant or sarcastic, brutal be cause of prideful infatuation, scornful and abusive, crooked and deceiving;

50. if appearing conceited with one's self and thus of the utmost contempt; taunting and angry: one should remain like a piece of wood.

51. The mind is [important] to me [only] for the sake of wealth, praise, glory; for the sake of retinue; and, again, for the sake of homage. Therefore, I remain like a stick of wood.

52. Being devoted to self-interest, my mind is cruelly opposed to the interest of others; but it is desirous of company, and it likes to talk. Therefore, I remain like a stick of wood.

53. It is without endurance, without energy, fearful, arrogant, and yet intent upon the welfare of its own kind. Therefore, I remain like a stick of wood.

54. When the mind is seen to be troubled, or attempting that which is fruitless, the hero ought always to restrain it firmly by means of the opposite behavior.

55. Resolved, serene, firm, respectful to whatever relates to the guru, with shame, with fear, mild, having as the highest object the satisfaction of others;

56. unwearied by the contradictory desires of the childish; but instead, full of pity for them, because this is from the arising of passion;

57. *always submissive to one's own will or to that of other creatures, in suitable circumstances; like a magical creation, without an opinion: Thus I bear whatever relates to the mind.*

58. *Having remembered the unique moment, obtained after a long time, having remembered again and again, I make the mind as firm in appearance as Mount Sumeru.*

59. *Pulled here and there by vultures greedy for flesh, the body does not resist. Why then retaliation? Why protect it, O Mind?*

60. *Why treat the body as one's own? If it is apart from you, then what to you is its decay?*

61. *You would not foolishly take as your own a filthy wooden doll. Why should I protect a stinking machine made of excrement?*

62. *By full use of the imagination take apart this leather bellows. With the knife of wisdom cut the flesh from a cage of bone.*

63. *Then, having taken apart the bones, behold the marrow within, and ask yourselves, "Where is its essence?"*

64. *Moreover, having searched carefully, and having seen that there is no essence of yourselves, now you ask, "Why should I still protect the body?"*

65. *The impure is not to be eaten by you. The blood is not to be drunk. The intestines are not to be sucked out. What will you do with the body?*

66. *For the sake of feeding vultures and jackals, one is intent upon the protection of this wretched body; yet it is only a servant of men.*

67. *Although the body may be guarded in this way by you, by death it is mercilessly cut off. Then it is given to the vultures. So what do you intend to do?*

68. *If a servant thinks that he will not continue, he is not given clothes or the like. The body, having eaten, will leave, so why do you waste [anything for it]?*

69. *Having given wages to him, now Mind! take care of your own interest, for all that one earns by serving for wages is not paid to him.*

70. *After making the intellect (buddhi) a ship in the body, because it comes and goes without refuge, so make the body move according to one's pleasure for the sake of the well-being of creatures.*

71. *The one who has brought his own self into subjection should have always a smiling countenance. He should discard frowns and suspicious looks, be the first to speak, be a friend of the world.*

72. *Such a one should not suddenly descend with loud cries, and break*

chairs, and so forth. Neither should he pound at a door; and it may be that he will not always take pleasure in noise.

73. *The crane, the cat, and the thief, walk without noise and without concern. They obtain their desired result. So should the ascetic always walk.*

74. *With bowed head he ought to accept the teaching of those who are able to direct others and who help without being asked. Always he ought to be the pupil of all.*

75. *He should praise, exclaiming "Excellent," for all that is well spoken. Having seen one achieving merit, he should encourage him with commendation.*

76. *One should discuss the virtues of others in private and repeat them with satisfaction; but when one's own praiseworthy character is mentioned, that should be considered as an appreciation of virtue in itself.*

77. *All achievement is for the sake of satisfaction, but even with money it is hard to grasp. I shall enjoy satisfaction only insofar as it is derived from the virtues achieved by the hard work of others.*

78. *In this way, no loss occurs to me, and hereafter there is great joy. But if one yielded to hatreds there would be the unpleasantness of hatreds here and great sorrow here*

79. *One should speak boldly directed sentences for the sake of clarity, which are pleasing to the mind, gratifying to the hearing, filled with compassion, and of a soft and gentle tone.*

80. *With the eye one should look honestly at beings, as if drinking together. Thus, by taking refuge with them I shall achieve Buddhahood.*

81. *Whether one experiences constancy and devotion, or hostility whether one experiences happiness or sorrow great good may ensue.*

82. *One should be clever, endowed with energy, and always self-reliant. There is to be no dependence upon anyone in any act.*

83. *The perfection of charity is superior to all else. One should not neglect the greater for the lesser value, even if the limits of conventional conduct must be ignored.*

84. *Thus enlightened, one ought to be constantly active for the sake of others. Even that which generally is forbidden is allowed to the one who understands the work of compassion*

85. *Only a moderate amount should be eaten, after sharing with those who have fallen into misfortune, and with those who are without protection, and with those engaged in a religious vow; because, with the exception of the three robes of the monk, one ought to sacrifice*

all.

86. One ought not to injure the body, which is the dwelling place of the true Dharma, for the sake of another. Only when it is preserved, may it speedily fulfill the desire of creatures.

87. One ought not to forsake life for a being whose motive of compassion (karuna) is impure; but for the one whose motive is worthy. In this way, having forsaken life, there is nothing lost.

88. One should not speak the doctrine to a person without dignity, or who [thinks himself] self-sufficient, or who wears a turban; and not to an [arrogant] person with an umbrella, a rod, or a sword, or whose head is covered.

89. The profound and exalted should not be spoken to the vulgar, nor to women without a man present. One should bring equal respect to the inferior and the superior Dharma [Hinayana and Mahayana];

90. but one ought not to yoke to the inferior Dharma that which is appropriate to the superior Dharma; and having forsaken good conduct, one ought not to deceive with scriptures (sutras) and mantras.

91. The display of a toothpick, the emission of snot, is not approved; and, also, urine and the like is forbidden in usable water and on good earth.

92. One ought not to eat with the mouth full, with noise, or with the mouth open. The foot ought not to be pendant, nor should one fold the arms together.

93. One ought not to take a journey lying down or 'sitting with another's woman. Having seen and investigated all that is disapproved by the world, he should avoid it.

94. One ought not to use a finger to point. Rather respectfully he ought to use his full right hand even if he should point out a road.

95. One ought not to make noise, throwing his arms about; but when one is a trifle hurried a snap of the fingers may be made. Otherwise one might be uncontrolled.

96. One ought to lie on a couch like the Lord in Nirvana, facing the proper direction, thoughtful, and quick to arise according to command.

97. The rule of conduct taught by the Bodhisattvas is immeasurable; but one should always practice that conduct which leads to the purification of the mind.

98. Three times by night and by day one should utilize the three aggregates. By means of this, and by taking refuge in the Conquerors and in the Awakening Mind, the rest of one's faults are

quieted.

99. *Whatever circumstances one may experience, either caused by himself or by others, he zealously should practice whatever rules apply just then.*

100. *There is nothing, once they accept the discipline, which is not to be understood by the sons of the Conqueror. There is nothing which exists which is without merit to such a one.*

101. *Both directly and indirectly one must act only for the welfare of sentient beings. One should bend everything to their welfare and to their Enlightenment.*

102. *One should never abandon, even for the sake of one's life, a good friend who holds to the law of the Bodhisattva and who is skilled in the ways of the Mahayana.*

103. *As indicated by the Sri Sambhavavimoksa one ought to practice whatever is taught by the masters. From the recitation of sutras, both this one and others, that which has been spoken by the Buddha is to be known.*

104. *The rules are seen in the sutras. Because of this, one should recite the sutras. And in the Akasagarbah-sutra one should examine the root sins.*

105. *The Siksasamuccaya certainly is to be looked at again and again, because good conduct is explained there in detail.*

106. *Or else, in the meantime, one should consult the Satrasamuccaya, as a compendium; and [its] companion composed by the noble Nagarjuna [should be studied] zealously.*

107. *After you have learned in the discipline wherein you are prohibited and wherein you are commanded, you ought to act for the purpose of protecting the mind in all situations.*

108. *This, then, in brief, is the mark of total awareness (sarhpraianya): the continual examination of the state of one's body and of one's mind.*

109. *Thus I read with the body, but what good is speaking and reading? What good is a mere medical treatise to the sick?*

Rinpoche's Commentary on Mindfulness

We could say mindfulness (Tib. *trenpa*) means not forgetting, not forgetting Mahamudra, not forgetting mind as it is. The attentiveness that we are speaking about is the right-up-to-the-moment attentiveness,[13] the present, active knowledge that becomes possible by way of mindfulness. So if one has mindfulness, then attentiveness can develop, and if one's mindfulness declines, then one's attentiveness is not possible. Also, when we talk about vigilance (Tib. *sheshin*) we are looking at our mind from the point of view of asking or inquiring: Are faults of this sort or that sort arising? Is samadhi or the stability of meditation declining? One watches to see that disadvantageous aspects don't creep into one's meditation.

Mindfulness and attentiveness are important at all times, and the reason for that is very simple. If they are present, then faults will not arise; and if they are absent, then faults will arise. This is explained by Shantideva who compared disturbing emotions to bandits. If you are protected by people who are strong, then thieves and murderers cannot possibly do you any harm; they see that you are well protected and they will not injure or steal from you. However, if your guardians become lazy or stupid or weak, then burglars can sneak in and harm you and steal whatever they want. So, Shantideva said, it is like that with regard to thoughts and disturbing emotions in that so long as you are well protected by mindfulness and attentiveness, then thoughts and disturbing emotions cannot take control. But as soon as mindfulness and attentiveness slacken or are abandoned, immediately disturbing emotions arise, many thoughts arise, and they bring much trouble by blocking and covering over whatever good qualities there are. For that reason it is important to adhere to mindfulness and attentiveness at all times.

Vigilance tames the mind, which is to say it subdues the disturbing emotions and keeps one from doing things that cause others to give rise to aggression, envy, pride, and so forth. At the same time, vigilance dispels the joy one takes in what are actually harmful things, which is to say it prevents one from seeing attachment and aggression as good characteristics. Vigilance enables one to see such things as faulty and therefore not to enjoy them. It is vigilance that understands the reasons why dharma is beneficial. And it enables one to take delight in the dharma, preventing one from disliking the dharma. In sum, mindfulness, attentiveness, and vigilance are extremely important to the practice of meditation and they enable one's meditation practice to develop further and further.

Mindfulness

Generally speaking, mindfulness means not forgetting about the object upon which one is meditating. The text says, "As for mindfulness, it enables one not to forget the meaning that one is seeking to accomplish." It keeps your mind on the point that you are contemplating in your meditation, and it maintains clarity within your meditation. In particular, the sutra called the *Sutra Requested by the Student Who Had a Jewel upon the Crown of his Head,* called the Tsugna Rinpoche sutra in Tibetan, points out the different functions of mindfulness. One of these is: "Through mindfulness, delusions do not arise." Because we have become so well accustomed to disturbing emotions and have established such strong predispositions and habitual tendencies in that direction, through the force of those habitual tendencies, disturbing emotions will arise. But if we sustain mindfulness, then those disturbing emotions of desire, hatred, pride, and so forth do not arise. Secondly, through mindfulness, we do not become involved in demonic activity. These two are related as root and branch. First of all, through mindfulness, we protect our mind so that disturbing emotions do not arise. Once disturbing emotions do not arise in the mind, then the activities of body and speech do not go in the direction of demonic action (Skt. *mara*). Thirdly, through mindfulness, we do not stray from the correct path. That is to say mindfulness keeps us on the path that leads to genuine benefit. In this way, mindfulness can be understood as a doorway.

In the Buddhist tradition, when we talk about mind, we often talk about mind and mental factors, mental factor being "that which arises from mind." Through the force of mindfulness, the mind does not go in an unvirtuous direction. For that reason, the text says, "We should exert ourselves at genuine mindfulness." To speak a bit more about mind and mental factors, what we're talking about is very subtle kinds of thought. In fact, mindfulness is itself one of these mental factors, and it has the particular aspect of causing one not to forget whatever one is trying to pay attention to. Mindfulness has the role of keeping the mind on the point that one is meditating. If we guard our mind well with mindfulness, then we will not wander from it. We will not sink into dull states of mind or wild states of mind. When we have understood the dharmata that is the mind's way of being, then through the power of mindfulness we will not stray from that to something else. Thus, mindfulness is critical in guarding the realization that comes about as the insight of Vipashyana.

Vigilance

Vigilance (Tib. *sheshin*) has a sense of presently knowing what's going on in your mind and looking very closely at it. The text says that first you have to establish mindfulness. When you have established mindfulness, then this quality of vigilance, knowing at the present moment what's going on in your mind, can arise. Vigilance arises in dependence upon mindfulness. It inspects or examines the activities of the three doorways of body, of speech, and of mind. And this vigilance knows what to accept and what to reject. So this vigilance is critical for nourishing a healthy state of mind. There is a passage from Shantideva's *Bodhisattva's Way* which says very simply, "Once you have established mindfulness, and mindfulness is serving the function of guarding your mind, then vigilance (or knowing what's going on in your mind at that moment), will naturally come about."

It is important to rely upon mindfulness and vigilance because their particular activities in the context of Mahamudra meditation sustain one's realization of the mind's way of being and brings forth the enhancement of that realization. Mindfulness and vigilance very precisely enables one to know what to accept and what to reject. Without mindfulness and vigilance, different faults arise. In the *Bodhisattva's Way* it says that if you do not have vigilance, then your practice of listening to the dharma, reflecting upon its meaning, and meditating upon what you have understood will really not go anywhere. It will turn out to be a waste of time. And your good qualities will not increase and you will not be able to retain what you have accomplished.

When you have proper mindfulness and vigilance, then the self-restraint or carefulness of which we spoke earlier can arise in the continuum of your mind. What exactly is this self-restraint or carefulness? It knows when delusion is arising. It sounds the alarm. It says, "Oh, I think there's some delusion coming around here." And then you can respond to that appropriately.

Mindfulness as the Root

Mindfulness is the root of attentiveness and mindfulness is the root of vigilance. If one sustains mindfulness, then meditation, samadhi, and all good qualities will increase straight away. If mindfulness declines, then so will one's meditation and one's good qualities. Therefore, the siddhas of the Kagyu lineage talk about "holding mindfulness." This notion of holding mindfulness is explained with the metaphor of the shepherd. Mindfulness allows one to remain within the state of meditation. Just as when sheep wander into a place where there are fierce animals that would devour them, then the shepherd will bring the sheep back. Or if a sheep wanders to a precipitous place, the shepherd will bring it back to a place that has water and grass, where it will be happy and want to stay. In the same way when the mind strays from meditation, it is mindfulness that brings it back to meditation and places it in the relaxation of meditation so that one can enjoy its benefits.

Mindfulness is vital to the practices of listening, contemplating, and meditating upon the meaning of the dharma. Furthermore, it is important for sustaining meditation because it focuses the mind into one-pointedness. This means that it prevents the mind from becoming distracted into some other activity. If you do not have mindfulness, then you will also lose the purpose that you are attempting to accomplish. You will become confused and get lost. So mindfulness is important if you're going to practice meditation. If you don't have it, then you lose the meditation. It's mindfulness that tells you whether or not your meditative stabilization is coming along well or not. If you have mindfulness, then you can maintain your meditative stabilization; if you do not, then it gets lost. For that reason, it's important.

Mindfulness in Meditation

When we are practicing meditation, we are working on the level of the sixth mental consciousness. We meditate and develop this quality of stability of resting with the object. In the development of Shamatha, mindfulness and awareness are essential. When we speak about the mind, it has two aspects: mind (Tib. *sem*) and *mental factors* (Tib. *sem yung*). The mind in this case is the central awareness, the knowing quality. Mental factors are, figuratively speaking, companions that give the mind its color and flavor. What we understand as thoughts are actually these mental factors. What actually looks at the object? It is the mental factor that is called mindfulness (Tib. *dren pa*). Mindfulness is the quality of non-distraction. Without such mindfulness there can be no meditation or samadhi. When there is such mindfulness, mind does not wander and stray. If mindfulness fails, then the mind wanders. What is it that knows whether or not the mind has wandered? It is the quality of alertness (Tib. *sheshin)*. This quality of alertness, which has the sense of knowing in the present, knows that the mind has wandered. These two are of great importance when one wishes to practice meditation. The great Shantideva praised their importance by saying that mindfulness and awareness should be valued by meditators more than their own lives. He said, "I place my palms together to express my respect for mindfulness and awareness and for those who have developed them."

When one first practices Shamatha, it is said one's mind tends to resemble a crazy elephant who runs amok and does a lot of harm whether one uses the body of a deity as the object of one's observation or holds one's attention on the inhalation and exhalation of the breath, one needs to hold one's mind to it and stay with it. How does one go about tying one's mind to the object of observation? You have an elephant, you use a rope and tie the elephant to a stake to keep it from running all over. With the mind, one uses mindfulness as one's rope and one ties this crazy mind to the object of observation.

For a beginner to achieve an excellent Shamatha is rather difficult because the mind tends to wander. For that reason, mindfulness and alertness are extremely important. If one's mind has various thoughts, one is aware of those thoughts and with mindfulness one can return one's mind to the object of observation in a relaxed way. Mind can be divided into consciousness and mental factors. In this case, mindfulness is regarded as a mental factor which is a perceiving subject, with the mind being its object. In other words, mindfulness is looking at the mind to see whether or not it has wandered. The Tibetan word for "mind" is *sem*, with the Sanskrit word being *chitta*. The Tibetan word for "mental factors" is *sem yung* which literally means "arising from the mind" or "arising with the mind." Mind or *sem* has six consciousnesses; sometimes one speaks about eight consciousnesses.[14] The six are the eye, the ear, the nose, the tongue, the body sensations, and the mental consciousnesses. These consciousnesses know their objects individually so that eye consciousness sees visible forms, ear consciousness hears sounds, nose consciousness experiences smells, and so on with mental consciousness being where many different thoughts appear and are integrated. The mental factors occur with those main consciousnesses.

There are several types of mental factors. Some are always there and always accompany each consciousness. Others exist sometimes, but not other times. Mental factors that always accompany the mind are pleasure and pain. Sometimes the feeling is strong, sometimes it is weak, but the feeling accompanies every consciousness. Similarly, discrimination is a mental factor that knows what things are and recognizes the details of things. This consciousness accompanies all the six consciousnesses because every consciousness has some quality of discrimination. The mental factors that occasionally appear are, for instance, mindfulness, awareness, faith, and confidence. These are said to be beneficial mental factors and when they accompany the mind, the mind is a favorable mind. Not being permanent, sometimes they are there and sometimes not. There are also mental factors that are not beneficial such as passion, aggression, envy, or the wish to harm. When these negative factors accompany the mind, then that mind is not favorable.

The mental factor of mindfulness (Tib. *dren pa*) keeps one from forgetting the object. As long as mindfulness is present, one does not forget the object, and when mindfulness is absent, one does forget the object. If one then places one's mind back on the object, thinking, "I am not going to let my mind wander again," with the absence of mindfulness, the mind will again fall under the influence of other things. So it is important that mindfulness be there all the time to keep the mind from wandering.

Along with mindfulness, alertness (Tib. *seshin*) is also very important, since it brings the mind back. Mindfulness is a mental factor that looks at the mind itself to see whether or not the mind is staying with the object. This allows the mind to rest within a state of relaxation. Mindfulness then serves as a guardian of that state. The nature of the relationship between mindfulness and alertness is that if mindfulness is present, it brings alertness along with it. And if mindfulness is absent, then alertness doesn't happen either. So it is very important to develop these both and not lose them.

Protecting mind from the disturbing emotions and discursive thought can be compared to protecting oneself from thieves. Thieves will know not to attack a strong, powerful, well-disciplined and attentive person. Rather they will attack someone who is sloppy and lazy and weak. Mindfulness and awareness make one strong, attentive, and well-disciplined. With these one cannot be robbed by disturbing emotions and discursive thought. Someone who lacks mindfulness and awareness is the one who will be plundered. What is stolen are the roots of beneficial factors that exist within one's mind. With mindfulness and awareness, the disturbing emotions will have no hope of being able to rob you and will just give up.

The mind should be protected from disturbing emotions and discursive thought that are compared to thieves. Thieves will know not to attack a strong, powerful, well-disciplined, and attentive person. Rather they will attack someone who is sloppy and lazy and weak. So, mindfulness and awareness make one strong and attentive and well-disciplined. With these one cannot be robbed by disturbing emotions and discursive thought. Someone who has no such mindfulness and awareness is the one who will be plundered. What is stolen is the roots of beneficial force that exists within one's mind. If one has such mindfulness and awareness, then those disturbing emotions will have no hope of being able to rob you and will just give up.

Mindfulness is regarded as impermanent, as a temporary, rather than a permanent mental factor. But, suppose you were to sit down and practice meditation for an hour and exert yourselves, develop good mindfulness, then when you got up, you didn't have such mindfulness. That is all right, because gradually you get used to it and as you get used to it, you become familiar with it, and then it doesn't take such effort to have mindfulness. It will arise effortlessly of its own force.

Questions

Question: I lose my mindfulness after I have had it. But I also see that I become more familiar with mindfulness and that is beneficial.

Rinpoche: No, it doesn't just disappear. When you cultivate qualities such as faith, devotion, and wisdom or prajna, they become more and more stable and clear. They don't just suddenly disappear one day. You can think about it in comparison to the way you go to school and develop prajna. You go year after year and you develop knowledge and intelligence. You don't just suddenly wake up one day and find they are gone. When you go to school, you are developing prajna. When you practice meditation you are developing mindfulness and awareness. In the same way that when you go to school to train your prajna and it doesn't just suddenly disappear. So, when you are trained in meditation and develop your mindfulness, you don't just wake up to find that your mindfulness has just completely disappeared. Sometimes if you have been in some real hardship and are quite tired, it is difficult to maintain mindfulness. But as you meditate more and become more familiar with the good qualities and benefits of meditation, then it is easier for that mindfulness to remain. If you think about the discussion of the nine stages of resting the mind and what was presented in terms of pacifying the mind and taming the mind, the fifth and sixth stages, look back at those. You will see some notions about how mindfulness becomes very steady.

Chapter 6

The Perfection of Patience

The Bodhisattva's Way of Life consists of ten chapters with the three first chapters being more important than the others. The first chapter explains the benefits ensuing from bodhichitta. The second chapter explains confession, and the third chapter concerns the full acceptance of bodhichitta and the way in which one actually takes the bodhisattva vows. For this reason, I will not go into the previous two chapters that explain conscientiousness and awareness or mindfulness.

The first three chapters explain how we arouse awakening mind. The next three chapters explain how we prevent bodhichitta from decreasing after it has been aroused or engendered. The last three chapters explain how to increase awakening mind. This chapter is concerned with the methods from preventing bodhichitta from deteriorating. The main obstacle which causes deterioration of awakening mind is anger.

The remedy for this is patience the subject of this chapter.

In interviews, many people have asked me how to counteract anger. This seems to be a great obstacle for the majority of practitioners. Therefore I hope that this explanation on the sixth chapter which explains patience will be of great help for everyone.

The reason it's necessary to relinquish anger is given in the following verses:

1. *Hostility destroys all the moral conduct, charity, and reverence of the Buddhas, which has been achieved in thousands of eons.*
2. *No evil is equal to hatred, and no austerity is equal to patience. Therefore one ought diligently to cultivate patience by a variety of means.*
3. *He does not achieve a tranquil mind, nor attain the joy of pleasure or of sleep or of constancy, when he walks with the arrow of hatred within his heart.*
4. *Those whom he honors with profit and regard, even those who are dependent upon him, they, too, desire to injure that Lord who has hatred as an ugly characteristic.*
5. *Even friends shrink from him, and no gift serves him. In short, the angry-minded man has no way whatever by which to be happy.*
6. *But the one who with perseverance destroys anger; by knowing the enemy, by realizing that he creates only sorrows, this one is happy here and*

elsewhere.

7. *When my portion is unhappiness, which is caused by wrongdoing and frustration of desire, arrogant hatred afflicts me.*

8. *Therefore I will destroy hatred's nourishment, because that enemy has no other purpose than my destruction.*

9. *My joy will not be disturbed, even by the occurrence of the most frustrating event, because even in unhappiness, there is nothing which can adversely affect a virtue which one truly desires.*

10. *In this way, if there is a remedy, what then is unhappiness? If there is no remedy, what then is unhappiness?*

These verses explain why it's necessary to relinquish anger. We might decide not to become angry ever again. However, even though we think this, it's not possible to follow through and anger will arise. We simply cannot decide that, "Anger will never arise in my mind again." Because we do not have such control over the course of events. So it isn't really possible to prevent anger from arising by simply suppress it. In terms of Western psychology, if one tries to suppress an emotion such as anger, many problems will ensue. Eastern psychology agrees to this. Trying to suppress an emotion like anger will result in an unhealthy state of mind. In terms of Eastern psychology we first develop an understanding of the problems ensuing from anger. After understanding this, we will naturally develop a dislike for anger.

If we haven't thought about anger and its result, then when we are harmed by someone, we become very angry. On the other hand, if we have examined anger, then we will realize that the harm brought about by our enemy is very slight in comparison with the harm ensuing from an angry mind. Therefore, we should understand that in one's own anger is the actual enemy, not the person that has harmed us. Having identified the real enemy, we should then resolve to overcome anger, if anger is overcome, then happiness and comfort will result. We should also think of the negative qualities resulting from having given up anger and aggression. Thinking this, we will develop aspiration to relinquish anger, which results in happiness and comfort for ourselves and all other beings. In this way, we then develop an aspiration towards giving up anger.

Relinquishing anger is done by means of contemplating patience. There are three things which cause anger:

11. *It is undesirable that there be sorrow, humiliation, reproach, or disgrace, for one's loved ones or oneself or, even, contrariwise, for one's enemy;*

Personal suffering, being disrespected, and being spoken to harshly causes anger. If the people who treat us poorly are happy and respected, and praised, we also becomes angry. So there are nine objects of meditation for developing patience. The first three relate to ourselves and these are personal suffering, disrespect, and harsh words. Next are personal suffering, disrespect, and suffering of persons dear to us. Finally, there is the person whom we despise not having nay suffering, disrespect, or receiving criticism. Then in relation to one's dear ones, and then the opposite things happening to one's enemies. So there are nine objects of focus in all.

Next, the actual practice of meditation on patience is explained. There are three types of patience. The first type of patience is dealing with and accepting suffering or what we could call forbearance. The main one is to overcome anger towards one's enemies. Second, there is forbearance with suffering. Third, there is patience in relation to practices that aim at realizing the true nature of phenomena.[15] This last one means we shouldn't become discouraged and think that we are not able to realize the true nature. We should be patient with ourselves and keep at the practice. Overcoming anger towards our enemies or persons we don't like is the main meditation with tolerating suffering and not becoming discouraged in practice being supplementary. Beginning with forbearance in the following verses:

12. *How difficult it is for happiness to be seized, while sorrow exists without effort. And still, escape is only by means of sorrow: Therefore make firm the mind!*

13. *The little sons of Durga, the Karnatas, endure in vain the torture of burning, laceration, and so forth, for the sake of release. Why then am I cowardly?*

14. *There is nothing whatever which is difficult after repetition: So by the repetition of moderate pain, great pain may be endured.*

15. *Why do you see sorrow as profitless the pain caused by bugs and flies, hunger and thirst, and so forth; caused by a great itch, and the like?*

16. *One is not to be made tender by cold and heat, rain and wind, travels and disease, imprisonment and beatings; otherwise, pain will be increased.*

17. *Some fight all the more when they see their own blood; but some, when they have seen only the blood of others, become faint.*

18. *This has come from the strength or the weakness of the mind. Therefore, one ought to be invincible to sorrow. One ought to overcome pain.*

19. *Even in sorrow the enlightened one ought not to disturb the tranquillity of the mind; because he is fighting with the passions, and in warfare pain is trivial.*

20. *Some who receive enemy blows upon their breasts conquer their enemies.*

They are victorious heroes, but others are only slayers of the dead.
21. *And there is further virtue that is caused by the agitation of sorrow:*
    compassion in the cycles of rebirth, the loss of pride, the fear of evil, and
    delight in the Conqueror.

The second type of patience is with suffering, the main thing is to be able to abandon afflictions or disturbing emotions. To be able to obtain great results in one's dharma practice, one will have to go through many difficulties and one will needs diligence. When one encounters these difficulties, then one must be able to be patient with these difficulties. Otherwise, one will not be able to finally attain the fruition. So in order to be able to attain the ultimate result, one needs to have forbearance with the difficulties one encounters in one's practice.

The third type of patience is patience in relation to the dharma beginning with verses:

22. *I am not irritated by the bile and such, although these cause great sorrow.*
    How then can I be irritated by sentient beings? These also are irritated by
    causes.
23. *As this [bodily] pain arises, although not desired, so also anger forcibly*
    arises, although not desired.
24. *A man does not become angry by his own free will, after having thought, "I*
    am angry." And anger does not arise by intending to arise.
25. *Likewise, offenses and sins of various types, all arise from the power of*
    causation. Independence is not known.
26. *The thought, "I am born," is not related to the structure of causation. The*
    thought, "I was born," is not related to what is produced.
27. *The primary matter[16] which is so desired, and the self (atman) which is*
    imagined, are not produced by thinking, "I become."
28. *Verily, since there is nothing unoriginated (anutpanna), who can desire to*
    come into being? And because of pre occupation with sense-objects
    (visaya) one cannot even hope for cessation.
29. *And if the Absolute (atman) is like the sky, eternal and unconscious, it is*
    clearly inactive. If it is in a state of non-attachment amongst causes
    (pratyaya), how can the changeless act?
30. *In regard to the Atman, what does it do in the time of action which connects*
    it to action? When there is a relationship based on the notion that the
    3,tman acts, where is the connection? How can there be a relationship
    between the two?
31. *Thus all is subject to a cause, which cause likewise is not self-caused. How,*
    then, can one be angry with beings who move and speak as a magical
    creation?
32. *It may be thought, because resistance [to anger and the like] is not*

dependent [on anything], who and what can resist? But since that which is dependent is the very fact of being dependent, the cessation of sorrow may be conceived.

33. *In this way, when one has seen either friend or foe behaving improperly and has understood that there is such and such a cause for this, he will remain happy.*

We should then consider the reasons for engendering this type of patience which is related to dharma. Generally speaking, people do not have control over the course of events that they can prevent anger from arising. If we then consider those who want to do harm to us, they are not the real enemy. The true enemy is our own anger. So we should consider anger in this way and develop an understanding of the faults and defects ensuing from giving rise to anger or aversion.

There is no being that is able to control the course of events. All beings are under the influence of various factors or conditions. We should then understand that when our enemy harms us, this is due to his confusion. It is because he or she is not in control because of his or her anger. Therefore there is no real reason to be angry with this enemy or persons who tries to harm us.

So whomever harms us, whether it is an enemy or relative or close friend, we shouldn't think bad of that person. Instead, we should think that this person can't really help what he or she is doing, since the person in question has no control over the course of events. The person who harms or slights us is, after all, influenced by disturbing emotions that caused them to act that way towards us. So in such a situation, we should try to relax rather than becoming angry.

The first type of patience of being patient with enemies is described in the following verses:

34. *If the success of all creatures came by means of their own desire, none would be sorrowful, for no one desires sorrow.*

35. *Yet they damage themselves with thorns, because of self infatuation, because of the loss of a loved one, because of anger, because of coveting a faraway woman, and such like.*

36. *Some destroy the self by hanging or by falling; by poisoned, unwholesome food, and so forth; or by doing that which is without merit.*

37. *If thus subjected to passion, they even destroy their beloved self, how can there be any sparing of the bodies of others?*

38. *For those who are made mad by passion, and turned to self-destruction, there is only pity. How can anger arise?*

39. *If the nature of fools is that which causes injury to others, a reaction of*

anger is no more appropriate for them than for the fire whose nature it is to burn.

40. *And, on the other hand, if this hatred is accidental, and beings are lovely by nature, then this anger is likewise as inappropriate as if it were against the air, which is filled with acrid mist.*

41. *If one becomes angered at the motivation, which prompts someone to throw a stick or the like at a person, he too is motivated by hatred; but for me let there be hatred of the hate.*

42. *Formerly, I too inflicted such pain upon beings: So it is also suitable for me, one who has done injury to beings!*

43. *His sword and my body are the double means of making sorrow. The sword is seized by him, the body by me: Against which is one angry?*

44. *It is a boil, shaped like a body, unable to bear being touched, which has been seized. Because I am blinded by desire, I stagger: Why be angry?*

45. *I do not desire sorrow, I desire the cause of sorrow. I am a fool. Since sorrow comes from my own offense, why should I be angry elsewhere?*

46. *Since the forest of sword [razor sharp] leaves and the birds of hell are engendered by my own Karma, why, then, be angry?*

47. *Those who injure me have been prompted by the impulse of my Karma, because of which they go to hell: Surely they are destroyed by me.*

48. *By recourse to them, my great evil is destroyed through being patient. By recourse to me, they go to the long anguish of hell.*

49. *I am injurious to them and they are good to me. When this situation is reversed, why are you angry, you who are foul-minded?*

50. *If I do not go to hell it will be because of my reserve of good qualities. What is it to others if I have been protected by myself?*

51. *If I engage in retaliation, others are not thereby protected, and yet my [Bodhisattva] career is forsaken, with the result that the wretched are lost.*

So in all, there are eighteen verses that explain this first type of patience. As already mentioned all beings lack freedom and control over the course of events. We should develop patience or meditate on patience by concentrating on this again and again. It is a fact that there is no being that desires suffering, so if beings had freedom to choose, then there wouldn't be any suffering since there is a choice. We all know that beings suffer, so we can understand that there is no such choice. That is in relation to suffering. In this particular context, we are considering anger which is a specific emotion not desired by anyone, but it does arise in the minds of beings because they have no choice or freedom. Thinking in this way, we should develop patience.

So beings have no freedom or choice whatsoever and are totally under the influence of various factors, such as the disturbing emotions. Most human beings value themselves as the most important person.

Though there are those that because of being greatly disturbed, for example, commit suicide. However, an angry person could harm us at any point. When this happens, we should think that it's improper to become angry in return, and instead try to develop compassion for him or her.

The second reason for it being improper to give rise to anger is in terms of being harmed by someone. Individuals are naturally concerned with their own welfare and will do anything to bring about personal comfort which might harm others in the process. In actual fact, when harmed by an individual there is no real reason for being angry with that person. An example is fire which naturally burns. If we get too close or sticks our hand into the fire, we will be burned. But we shouldn't become angry with the fire because heat is just on of the characteristics of fire. If we sit beside the fire and relax, we won't get burned. Similarly, we should understand that ordinary individuals naturally act in the way described, and therefore there is no reason to be angry with them. If we are harmed by somebody, we should just withdraw and relax, and not respond to their aggression. And in this way, the harm will be pacified. There's no reason for becoming angry with the person. It is his own anger that pushes him to act in this way, so we should not become angry with his anger.

If we are harmed by an enemy, for example, stabbed with a knife, maybe we would get sick and as a result suffer. Again, it's improper to become angry with the enemy, because the suffering is brought about by the weapon. Without such a weapon, we wouldn't have this physical suffering. On the other hand, there would also be no physical suffering if we had no physical body. So the weapon with which we are harmed and our body both are the causes for our suffering. In fact, it's not the enemy. So maybe we should get angry with the weapon or our own body.

The cause for ourselves being harmed by an enemy is karma accumulated in the past by ourselves. It's for that reason we are harmed. So we are responsible for what takes place due to the power of our own personal karma. In the future, the enemy having harmed us will come to suffer greatly, maybe be reborn in the hell realm. So in this situation, rather than becoming angry, we should develop patience. In fact, if we are able to do this, our enemy has benefited us because we have the opportunity to develop patience and accumulate great and vast virtue. As a result of this we will experience happiness and comfort. So, in actual fact, the enemy has benefited us.

In terms of practice we should aim at accumulating merit. The supreme method for doing this is contemplating and developing patience.

It is not possible to practice this without someone harming us because if we aren't harmed, then there is no reason really for contemplating patience. So, in actual fact, those who harm us are the supreme support for us developing patience. So in fact, our enemies are our main benefactors.

There are two methods to accumulating merit. One is to practice generosity and another is to develop patience. Practicing generosity is very easy since it's not difficult to find someone to be generous towards. It's more difficult to find somebody to be patient with, if we don't harm someone ourselves, then in fact, there wouldn't be anyone harming us. So when encountering such an individual, we should realize that in actual fact we are very fortunate.

2. Patience with those who slander us

We will now discuss the second kind of patience of patience toward persons who criticize us. This is covered in the following verses:

52. *The mind, because it has no form, cannot be destroyed by anyone in any place; but because it hinges upon the body, it is oppressed by the suffering of the body.*
53. *That hoard-humiliation, harsh language, and disgrace does not trouble the body. Why, 0 mind, are you angry because of it?*
54. *Whatever the dislike which others have for me, how can it consume me, either here or in another birth? For what reason should it be disliked by me?*
55. *It is not desirable for me to obtain something, if the necessary action involves a moral obstacle to acquiring it; my acquiring will vanish here, but my evil will remain steadfast.*
56. *Immediate death is better for me than a long life improperly lived; because even after having lived a long while, the sorrow of death comes to me anyhow.*
57. *The one who has enjoyed pleasure for a hundred years in sleep is awakened; and another who has been happy for an instant is awakened.*
58. *Surely the awakening destroys the pleasure of both. So it is the same at the time of death for the one who has lived long and for the one who has lived a short while.*
59. *Having received many advantages and having enjoyed pleasures for a long time, I shall depart as if plundered, empty-handed and naked.*
60. *By the advantage of being alive I achieve both merit and the waning of evil, but surely for the one who is angry because of this advantage, there is evil and the waning of merit.*
61. *If even the well-being for which I live is lost, what good is the life, which*

consists wholly in doing that which is unworthy?

62. *If you know that hatred destroys creatures by censure, why, then, as dishonor is done to another, does not wrath arise within you?*

63. *You have patience towards those who criticize, whenever the criticism is directed to others: But you have no patience with one who raises the question of your own shortcomings.*

It concerns this idea about disrespect, harsh speech, unpleasant words, criticism being belittled.

It is meaningless to become angry when someone makes disrespectful or belittling statements about you. For example, if someone attacks you physically, then, it is quite normal for the individual to develop some anger at being physically attacked. But even cruel words showing disrespect are unpleasant to hear, but the words will not hurt you. So it is not really proper to develop anger against merely words. One could still argue, "Yes, critical words do not really affect me, but being disrespectful to me, belittling me and my friends is not convenient or comfortable." But again, whether the other people like you or dislike you cannot affect you actually. So that is an explanation on developing patience with unkind words, disrespectful or belittling words.

3. Patience with Those Who Insult the Dharma

The third kind of patience is to have patience with those who insult the dharma or hurt spiritual teachers, relatives or friends is discussed:

64. *In the destruction and the cursing of images and stupas of the true Dharma, hatred does not affect me. Likewise, there is no pain for the Buddha or the like.*

65. *In the injuries of dear ones teachers, kinsmen, and so forth having seen, as before, the origin of causation, one ought to suppress anger.*

66. *Pain, whether inflicted consciously or unconsciously, is assured for embodied beings. Since this pain is beheld [only] in consciousness, endure this notion of pain.*

67. *Because of infatuation some offend. Others, also infatuated, are angry. Which of these do we call faultless? Which do we call guilty?*

68. *Why did you previously act in such a way that you are oppressed in this same way by others? All are dependent upon Karma. Who am I to alter this?*

69. *But thus enlightened, I strive for the merit by which all will become kind to one another.*

70. *A house is burning and the fire has fallen on a neighboring house wherein*

straw and other inflammables may be ignited; obviously they ought to be removed and pulled away.

71. *In like manner, when the mind is burnt by con tact with the fire of hatred, that fire immediately should be extinguished, out of fear that one's merit may be consumed.*

72. *If one who is to die is saved by cutting off a hand, why is he unfortunate? If one is saved from hell by human sorrows, why is he unfortunate?*

73. *If today one is not able to suffer even this measure of sorrow, why is anger, the cause of pain in hell, not restrained?*

74. *By reason of anger, I have been oppressed in hell thousands of times, and what I have done has been neither to my benefit nor to the benefit of others.*

75. *This is not such a sorrow, and it will create great benefit. One should be glad of the sorrow that takes away the sorrow of the world.*

For example, patience is necessary when we become angry against those who destroy images of buddhas or other enlightened beings. We become angry when people destroy stupas, and when they destroy the dharma. But it's not necessary to become angry with them because these images and teachings are simply symbolic objects of confidence in Buddhism. So those who destroy stupas and the sacred dharma will not actually harm or affect the enlightened beings, nor will they harm the stupa or the dharma itself. So it is proper not to be angry at these persons.

This teaching of Shantideva is really quite current because the Communists destroyed the temples, monasteries, the sacred images, relics and stupas, and burned many sacred dharma texts in Tibet. Many people having heard of this have become angry towards these actions. But, based on this teaching, it is not proper to become angry for what they have done, what they have destroyed, because it did not actually hurt the enlightened beings, the dharma, and the religious objects themselves.

Likewise, we should not develop hatred or anger towards those who try to harm our teacher, lama, or our relatives or friends, because the person who tries to harm them too is under the influence of conflicting emotions, defilements, and ignorance. With the choiceless situation they have acted in that manner to harm those people knowing that they are very much under a disillusion. It is proper not to angry at them.

Several years ago someone asked me, "Didn't you develop any anger, dislike, hatred toward the Communists who invaded your country, destroyed your monastery, and drove you out of your native land?" Because of a lack of alertness, mindfulness, instability of mind one could become angry. But not really thinking deeply in accordance with the sacred dharma, one would say, "Yes, I was angry." But again, relating with the teaching of the dharma, there is no solid, firm being known as a "Communist." And the leader of the Communists is not one solid individual. But then there were some groups of armies who chased me and shot at me. I did not develop anger towards them because I do not know them and they did not know me. They shot at me because it was their job and it was my job to try to escape; so there was no hatred between us. This example explains fairly vividly the actual meaning what it means to relate with the dharma towards the enemy or towards those that try to harm our friends, relatives, so forth.

When an enemy expresses aggression or anger towards us, it's proper not to express anger back or react with anger or aggression because you must have done something to make the other person angry at you. So therefore, you are also involved in the interaction and problem. Knowing this, since you are not pure, you try not to become angry.

The next ten verses concern jealousy in which we become upset because someone has praised someone we don't like.

76. *If joy and happiness are obtained by praising the good qualities of others, why, 0 mind, are you not gratified?*

77. *Here is delight and happiness for you, an up-swelling of pleasure without reproach, and it is not forbidden. Because of these good qualities, this is the best way of attracting others.*

78. *But if the thought is not pleasing to you that another is happy, then one ought to abstain from wages, gifts, and so forth, and reject both visible and invisible [rewards].*

79. *When your merits are mentioned, you desire that others be happy; but when the merits of others are mentioned, you do not desire yourselves to be happy.*

80. *After you have cultivated the awakening mind, because of desiring happiness for all beings, why are you angry when beings seize happiness by them selves*

81. *Indeed, you wish Buddhahood and the worship of the three worlds for all beings. Why do you burn within after seeing them enjoy transient honor?*

82. *The one who nurtures those whom you should nurture is giving to you as well. Although you have found a living for your family, you are not gratified, you are angry!*

83. *What does he not wish for beings who wishes their Enlightenment? Where is his awakening mind who is angry at another's success?*

84. *If a gift is not received by you, but it remains in the house of the giver, it is not yours in any way. What is it to you if it is given or if it is not given?*

85. *Should another cover up his merits, kindnesses, and other good qualities? Should he not accept that which is offered? Speak of what does not make*

you angry!
86. Not only do you not grieve for the sin which you your self have done, but you want to be envious of others who have acted meritoriously.

For example, what we really wish for is that we always experience happiness and comfort. What we always try to avoid is suffering and pain. Suppose then that someone is praising your greatest enemy and if you are concerned that your enemies will become successful, more famous then you will become upset. Instead, when someone else is praising your enemy, if you rejoice at this and do not develop dislike or anger, then your mind will remain in peace. You will be able to maintain your comfort and pleasure out of the virtue of rejoicing upon those actions. So developing jealousy of the success or fame of our enemy, leads us to discomfort and pain. That pain is caused by yourselves, so it's meaningless, in short.

The next three verses concern the reverse situation:

87. If because of your desire, something unpleasant has befallen an enemy, why should it happen again? It will not happen just because of your wishing, or without a cause.
88. If this accomplishment were the result of wishing, what happiness would there be for you in his sorrow? Well being would be ill-being because of this, what other result?
89. This, indeed, is a terrible hook fixed by the fisherman, Passion. The guardians of hell, having bought you, will cook you there in jars.

Someone could try to impede your success and when this happens you shouldn't develop anger. It's not proper to rejoice at the misfortune or suffering of your enemy. If rejoicing at the misfortune or pain and suffering of your enemy leads you to happiness, then that would be something else. But it does not. It doesn't add to the misfortune of other person or to their pain and misery, but rather leads you to accumulate further negative karma. Since it does not do any good, one should not rejoice at the downfall or the misfortune of your enemy.

Similarly, when other people try to prevent the success of your friends or relatives, naturally you develop anger upon those people who prevent those things. Once again it's not proper to express aggression towards them because developing anger would not do any good or solve the problem. So in the following verses:

90. Certainly praise, respect, and honor give me neither merit nor long life. Nor does strength give me health or physical well-being;

91. *yet the aim of intelligent men who [mistakenly] think that they know their own well-being is of this type. While seeking pleasure which is only mental, they resort to drink, gambling [and similar vices].*

92. *For the sake of honor they annihilate well-being, they destroy both well-being and the self. How are words to be eaten? And in death, whose is the joy?*

93. *As a child cries in pain when his sand castle is broken, so my own mind reacts at the loss of praise and fame.*

94. *Because it is without thought, the mere sound, "He praises me," is not an occasion of pleasure. That which causes pleasure is the thought, "Another is pleased with me."*

95. *Yet what to me is a stranger's pleasure, whether with me or because of another? His is the joy of pleasure, and even the smallest part of it is not mine.*

96. *If being happy is the result of his happiness, then I must always be happy. Why am I not happy in the happiness caused by the tranquillity of others?*

97. *Pleasure arises within me because of the thought, "I am praised by him": because of that which is unrelated! Such is only the behavior of a child.*

98. *The acceptance of praise destroys my security and my desire for emancipation, and it creates envy of those with good qualities, and anger at their success.*

99. *For this reason, those who have arisen to destroy my adulation, and so forth, are only preventing me, for the sake of my protection, from falling into injury.*

100. *Acceptance of honor is a bond which does not bring me to a longing for release. How can I hate those who release me from that bond?*

101. *How can I hate those who, authorized by the Buddha, as it were, have become obstacles when I am inclined to enter into sorrow?*

102. *Anger is not excused by thinking that another person has created an obstacle to one's merit. There is no austerity equal to patience. Surely, now is the occasion for it.*

103. *It is my own fault that I am not patient here. Moreover, it is I myself who create the obstacle when an occasion for virtue has arisen.*

104. *If something does not exist without something else in which its existence is discerned, the latter is its cause. How can it be called an obstacle?*

105. *The beggar who has approached at the proper time has made no obstacle to almsgiving, and the ascetic who is able to administer ascetic vows cannot be called an obstacle.*

106. *Beggars are easy to find in the world, but the one who will injure is hard to find; because if no one is wronged by me, no one will wrong me.*

107. *Gained without effort, discovered like a treasure in my house, my enemy is to be appreciated as a helper on the path to Enlightenment.*

108. *In this way the fruit of patience has been gained by him and by me. To him the first part is to be given, because he was the first occasion of patience.*

109. If the enemy is not to be honored because he does not intend the achievement of patience, how then can the true Dharma a mindless cause of accomplishment be honored?

110. It is said that he is intent upon harming me, but if the enemy is not honored, as if he were a physician who sought my health, how else is there patience?

111. Thus, contingent upon his evil intent, patience arises; and thus he is the cause of patience and he is to be honored by me as the true doctrine itself.

These verses concern having patience for those who try to jeopardize, harm, or prevent the success of our relatives and friends. Generally as ordinary beings we enjoy praise, fame, and success. But it is not very meaningful to enjoy these things, because praise and fame do not give us a long life or physical strength or good health. However, as an ordinary person we become unhappy when our success or fame diminishes. So dislike or anger should not be developed regardless of whatever situation we are in.

So it is really unnecessary to become angry or to enjoy the praise and fame. The example in the text is of a few children playing in the sand and building a beautiful sandcastle. However, the castle begins to collapse under their own weight and the children begin to cry and suffer at the experience of the ruined castles. But logically, having built a castle of sand was not of great benefit and when it collapsed it did not harm anything. So this shouldn't have caused suffering. A similar situation occurs with praise and success as well.

As a dharma practitioner our goal is to achieve realization through the practice of the dharma. The main key to the achievement of the dharma practice is developing patience within ourselves. To develop that patience, we need to have the object upon whom we can practice the patience. If we do not have anyone we dislike, who are we going to practice the patience on? For example, if there were a doctor who always treated us nicely, then there's no reason for us to really practice patience on the doctor. However, since patience is the main key to the success of the dharma practice, we need those persons whom we dislike or those persons who we feel have hurt us to practice on. Having understood that, we try to relate to our enemy as more like a spiritual friend. We even try to be very grateful to this enemy because they are the one who gives us the opportunity to practice patience on.

The importance of respecting our enemy is given in three reasons. The first reason explains that our enemy is the object or the fuel for establishing Buddha-qualities which is given in the following verses:

112. Because of this the Sage has said, "Beings are an opportunity; Conquerors also are an opportunity." And so, by honoring both, many have gone far towards perfection.

113. Since the discovery of the Dharma of the Buddha is occasioned both by [ordinary] beings and by the Conquerors, in what way are [all] being not equal to Conquerors?

114. The greatness of intention is not in itself, but rather in its effects. Because of this the magnanimity of beings is equal. Because of this, they themselves are equal.

115. Whatever is an honorable attitude of friendship, that is the magnanimity of the being. Likewise, whatever merit is by the grace of the Buddha, that is the Buddha's magnanimity.

116. In this way sentient beings are equal to Conquerors as particles which derive from the Buddhas Dharma, but they are not equal to Buddhas, who are oceans of good qualities wherein the particles are infinite.

117. If an atom of virtue, from the multitude which is the sole quintessence of virtue, is seen in anyone, the worship of the three worlds is not sufficient for such a one.

118. And among beings is found this excellent particle which arises from the Buddhas Dharma. In consideration of this particle, all beings are worthy of worship.

It is not proper for us to develop hatred, anger and disrespect for our enemies, being the field for accumulating merit for us.

To achieve a total awakening state of enlightenment requires two things or objects. First is developing faith, respect, and devotion to the buddhas, bodhisattvas, and enlightened beings. Without that development, one cannot achieve enlightenment. Second we need to develop compassion, *loving kindness*, and practice generosity towards all sentient beings. So sentient beings are an object that leads us to enlightenment. On the path many enlightened beings having practiced the loving kindness, compassion, and generosity to sentient beings to achieve enlightenment, and similarly, we should do the same.

The second reason for respecting our enemy is that when we develop respect, generosity, loving kindness, and compassion towards our enemy and all sentient beings, are pleasing the enlightened being as well as pleasing sentient beings. So practicing generosity and patience on our enemy and sentient beings is of great benefit to them as well as enlightened beings.

The third reason is given below:

119. And what of those immeasurable Benefactors and Friends without disguise? What other response can there be than abandoning self-interest for a sentient being?

120. They tear the body. They enter the Avici hell. For the sake of those who are there they do all that may be done. Even the one who has done the greatest injury is to be treated with all goodness.

121. How can I be arrogant to those Lords rather than dutiful to them? In that they are my own Masters they do not really consider what is in their own self-interest.

122. The great Sages are joyful when others are happy. They are concerned when others are in anguish. The satisfaction of all the great Sages is from that satisfaction. Also, in injury the Sages are injured.

123. When the body is wholly in flames there is no delight pertaining to desire; likewise, when a sentient being is in pain there is no means of pleasure for the Compassionate Ones.

124. In this way, whatever sorrow is inflicted by me upon a begotten being, because of it, sorrow is inflicted upon all the Great Compassionate Beings. I now confess that evil. The Sages, they who have been afflicted: May they forbear!

125. For homage of the Tathagatas I go now with my entire self into servitude to the world. May multitudes put their feet upon my head or slay me. May the Lord of the world be content.

126. The Compassionate Beings have taken possession of this entire world, there can be no doubt of it. Surely the Lords may be seen under the form of beings. How then can one be disrespectful?

127. Let this then be my vow: The honoring of the Tathagata, the complete fulfillment of my own well-being, the destruction of the sorrow of the world.

Practicing the Buddha-dharma will lead us to experience infinite, immeasurable bliss. Whatever happiness we have experienced out of the practice of dharma is made available to us by the Compassionate One, the enlightened being. Their kindness is immeasurable so we need to learn to repay the kindness of the buddhas or enlightened beings. Offering food, clothing and possessions to the enlightened beings does not totally repay their kindness because enlightened beings do not really long for food, clothing, or possessions. What enlightened wish us to do is to try to practice loving kindness, compassion, generosity, and patience with sentient beings. This is the proper way of repaying the kindness of the enlightened beings.

In short when you are helping the sentient beings, you are at the same time pleasing the enlightened beings. When you are harming sentient beings, essentially you are harming the enlightened beings. The example of this is trying to offer food to an individual who is caught in a fire.

So practicing patience is also a great offering to enlightened beings. It also is achieving your own purpose of bringing meaning to your life. Practicing patience will benefit others also so one should try not to become angry and practice patience.

The benefits of practicing patience and the problems with not practicing patience is given next:

128. As a single soldier of the king may mishandle a great multitude, because the multitude, looking away, is not able to retaliate;

129. since he is not really alone, and the king's power is his power; thus one should not dishonor any evil person who has offended,

130. because both the guardians of hell and the Compassionate Ones are his power. Thus one should honor beings in the manner of a servant before an irascible king.

131. What is an angered king able to do that may be like the anguish of hell which certainly will be experienced if one makes beings unhappy?

132. How can the pleasure of a king give anything which could be equal to that Buddhahood which certainly will be experienced by bringing happiness to any being?

133. Let one be a source of honor to beings that Buddhahood may result. Also, in this world, why will you not realize fortune, fame, and good position?

134 Abounding in the joy of the universal monarch (chakravartin), the patient man obtains beauty, health, rapture, and long life in the world of rebirth.

So here it is giving the example of that a "farsighted" person who is powerful and trusted by the king. For example, if a minor attendant of a king tried to harm this farsighted person, and this person simply does not react, knowing that he has the strong support of the king. Being a "farsighted" person, he would never react and harm back. Similarly, in a situation where sentient beings who are very powerless and try to harm us, it's proper not to return their harm with anger or dislike because by reacting to them, we are displeasing the buddhas and bodhisattvas. This will not only displease the buddhas, but it will accumulate negative karma which can result in being reborn in the lower realms. So one tries not to react or return harm to the powerless sentient beings, knowing that they are always loved by enlightened beings, buddhas and bodhisattvas.

So it is practical to really be concerned about sentient beings more than that of a powerful king. For example, if we do something to make a king displease us, he would punish you, but that would not lead to the experience of suffering and rebirth in the lower realm. But if we hurt sentient beings, that will lead us to accumulate negative karma, and a result of such karma as taking birth in lower realms and experiencing greater misfortune. Having understood this, we should be more frightened to harm sentient beings than to displease a king.

Questions

Question: How can we completely eliminate the disturbing emotions?

Rinpoche: One speaks of suppressing, for example, anger, and the antidote for this is patience. One develops patience by considering the result of what ensues from anger. Based on this one is able to suppress anger, but it's not uprooted. To abandon, for example, anger one then meditates on selflessness, that is, one meditates on the emptiness of all phenomena. In terms of the Vajrayana tradition, one meditates on *Mahamudra* or *Dzogchen*, and anger or any other affliction will be abandoned when the true nature of mind is realized. Then naturally these afflictions will have been pacified.

Question: What if you don't have any enemies?

Rinpoche: Well, it's difficult to find somebody who has no enemies at any time whatsoever. If one is able to develop patience thoroughly, then at that point, there will be no enemies.

In another chapter in this text, an example has been given in relation to that question. So, for example, one is not able to eliminate all one's enemies through anger, but it is through patience that all enemies are eliminated. The following analogy is given. If one walks around in bare feet, there are lots of stones on the ground which will hurt one. Now if one wanted to avoid being hurt by thorns, stones and so forth, one might consider covering the whole earth with leather. But in fact, that wouldn't be possible. But if one wore a pair of shoes and the soles of the shoes were covered with leather it would be the same as covering the earth with leather. Similarly, through anger one isn't able to eliminate all external enemies; but if one disciplines the inner enemy of one's own anger, all one's enemies will be eliminated.

Question: What if one acts very forceful and doesn't let a person do something which is very self destructive?

Rinpoche: This may not be anger but more determination. For example, if one wants to benefit a person and knows that person doesn't listen to what one says if one is gentle, then one might act in a wrathful way which actually benefits the person. But that's not the anger that we have been talking about because one's mind isn't bent on harming others.

Question: Can't anger be used for beneficial means?

Rinpoche: Sometimes it seems that there are occasions that you could use your anger as a means to be of some benefit. Such as when you use a strong word and that seems to help you. But actually anger is never beneficial. What has helped you here is your self-confidence. One should not mistake self-confidence and anger. Self-confidence is necessary, but anger does not lead to any benefit and there is no occasion for positive time for anger at all.

Question: It's very difficult to rejoice with people who are crazy, say the Communists. Can we at least try to talk with them and tell them that we don't think it was a positive action?

Rinpoche: As a Buddhist, that really depends upon the motive. When you are going to talk to the people who are praising the Communists, then you have to really examine what is your motive for talking to them be. What would the result of speaking to them. That is very important. If your motive is altruistic and if the result of speaking to them is free from anger, and it would benefit many beings in the future, then it's very proper to talk to them. However, if your motive is not pure and does not seem to have much benefit, then it's better to tolerate them and let it be. Remember there's patience which says not to really react with harmful actions.

Question: Could you please repeat the three reasons for respecting sentient beings.

Rinpoche: One is respecting the sentient beings because through such respect, we accumulate merit. Second is that through the respecting sentient beings, we are also pleasing the enlightened beings. And third is thinking of the benefits of the patience and the problems of not developing patience.

Question: How is it possible to rejoice if the Communists are praising what they did?

Rinpoche: You have to examine the motive of the person who is praising the Communists. If their motivation in praising the Communists is really towards benefiting sentient beings, then it should be accepted because the motive is altruistic. But if their motive in praising the Communists is to harm living things, then instead of developing anger, you must develop compassion for them.

Once again, I would like to make it clear with your question about rejoicing at the praise of your enemy and so forth. We must understand that we are speaking here as the personal enemy. If you have a personal enemy, then instead of really developing anger towards that individual who you hate and who he hates you, you try to develop joy at their success and develop some sense of compassion for them. But if there are persons who try to harm other living beings, we are not speaking of rejoicing at their actions. So this must be made clear.

Question: What do you do if it's not a long-term enemy but a very short-term enemy.

Rinpoche: The main thing here is that utilizing your wisdom or skillful means at that very moment. Of course, you have to defend yourselves and as using that skillful means, you can avoid any harm to yourselves. But at the same time, as a skillful means, you try not to develop anger or hatred upon that reaction.

Chapter 7

The Perfection of Enthusiasm

It is important to have diligence or enthusiasm or strength to practice the Dharma. When we practice Mahamudra meditation in the Kagyu lineage, we begin with the ordinary and extraordinary preliminary practices. We begin with the *four ordinary preliminaries* of contemplating the difficulty of obtaining a precious human birth, contemplating impermanence and death, contemplating karma and its results, and contemplating the drawbacks of samsara. This contemplation of the bodhisattva begins with:

> *1. Thus having become patient, one should become enthusiastic, for Enlightenment is gained by standing strong. Without perseverance there is no merit, as without the wind there is no movement.*
>
> *2. What is strength? Proper effort. What is its adversary? Sloth: attachment to contemptible things, despair, self-despising.*

We are able to accumulate merit only if we have diligence and it is the accumulation of merit that allows us to reach enlightenment. For this reason, it is important to develop diligence.

The Sanskrit word for "diligence" is *virya* and this word also implies "enthusiasm." Generally, enthusiasm or diligence means to do some kind of work. But there are various kinds of work. Some jobs are by nature good, and some are by nature unhealthy. To take upon ourselves activity that harms others is not being diligent in the context of the paramitas. If we take a job which is by nature unvirtuous, then this is considered laziness which is being attached to negative deeds. So we have to be aware that diligence means being happy doing what is by nature good and rejoicing in goodness of carrying out good deeds.

The Types of Laziness

> *3. Because one is unconcerned with the sorrow of rebirth, sloth arises through inertia, relish for pleasure, torpor, an eagerness to be protected.*
>
> *4. Scented by the hunters of disturbing emotions, caught in the net of birth, is*

not the very day when you are born a return to the countenance of death?
5. *Do you not see those of your own group dying according to their turn? And yet sleep is to you as the buffalo to the outcast (candala).*
6. *Being observed by Death, paths blocked in every direction, how can you enjoy eating? sleep? sensual pleasure?*
7. *As soon as death has assembled his tools he will come quickly. Having then forsaken your sloth, what will you do at that unseasonable time?*
8. *This remaining unfinished! This begun! This half done! Suddenly death appears. Thinking, "Alas! I am smitten,"*
9. *beholding your relatives in despair, their eyes red with tears, swollen by the shock of grief.*
10. *tortured, and [beholding also] the faces of the messengers of death, by the memory of your evil, hearing the roarings of hell, the shaking body smeared with the excrement caused by terror: What will you do?*
11. *Here you are filled with fear, thinking, "I am like a live fish [confined to be eaten]." How much more is the intense misery of hell to the evildoer?*
12. *O tender one, you suffer pain when touched by warm water. And having done hellish Karma, how can you remain at your ease?*
13. *O reward seeker, you are lazy! O greatly suffering, you are tender! O immortal, you are seized by death! Miser able one, you are destroyed*

The obstacle to diligence is laziness and there are three kinds of laziness. The first kind of laziness is being attached to doing what is unwholesome. The second kind of laziness is feeling no inclination to engage in spiritual practice. The third laziness is feeling that we are not able to actually accomplish anything by thinking, "someone like me cannot reach anything as great as enlightenment."

Of these three kinds of laziness, the second is the lack of an inclination to practice and this laziness expresses itself by us feeling that it is enjoyable to do things that are pointless. Also this laziness includes a craving for sleep.

When we come under the influence of laziness, we will not develop any desire to renounce samsara. The Buddha himself made the suggestion that contemplation of impermanence is the remedy for this laziness. By not knowing the nature of impermanence and the role it plays in our life, we will never be able to enter into the dharma. But if we contemplate the impermanent nature of phenomena, we will develop the inclination to do dharma practice. Thus it is said that impermanence acts as an entrance or a door into the dharma. The contemplation of impermanence also helps us along the path by encouraging us to practice. In fact, the Buddha said that thoroughly understanding impermanence is essential for achieving enlightenment.

14. Having reached the ship of manhood, cross the great river of sorrow. Fool! this is not the time for sleep. The ship is hard to find again.

The next verse shows how everyone has to die and how everyone will undergo all kinds of suffering at the time of death and also after death. When contemplating this, we soon realize that the only way to avoid the suffering of death is to practice the dharma. The example given is that when we want to cross a wide river, we need a boat. This precious human body is like a boat that can take us to the other side of the ocean of misery. It is the best possible vessel for making this journey. If we do not use this boat, then in the future we may not have it to cross over to the other shore. So for this reason there is not even time to sleep.

15. Having cast away the delight of the Dharma, the most noble course of endless delight, how is there delight for you in arrogance, derision, and such causes of sorrow?

16. Self-mastery: aiming at courage and achievement of power, identity of the self and others, and likewise, exchange of the self and others [are aspects of enthusiasm].

17. One is not to be fatigued with the thought, "Why should Enlightenment come to me?" The Tathagatha, the truth speaker, has uttered this truth:

18. Even those who formerly were gnats, mosquitoes, flies, and worms have obtained the uttermost Enlightenment, so very difficult to obtain, by reason of resolution and effort.

19. How much more am I, having been born a man, able to know advantage and disadvantage? Why shall I not obtain Enlightenment by·means of not abandoning the rule of the All-knowing?

20. If I am afraid because of the thought, "A hand or a foot or something must be lost," that is only due to a lack of discrimination in choosing between the important and the unimportant.

21. I can be cut, split, burnt, lanced repeatedly, for innumerable millions of eons and I will not become enlightened;

22. but this limited sorrow is productive of my complete Enlightenment. It is like the sorrow of extraction when one removes the pain of a buried arrow.

The next verse discusses how we should deal with the first kind of laziness which is the attraction towards unwholesome actions. We may believe that unwholesome actions bring us pleasure and feel that we cannot live without these kinds of pleasures. But when we investigate a little deeper, we see that there is no need for this attraction towards unwholesome activities. We begin to realize that true, enduring happiness is no other than engaging in the dharma and it is this dharmic activity which gives us an authentic happiness which is enlightenment. Without relying on the sacred dharma, there would be no way to reach true happiness.

We should be happy with those things which cause true happiness, and not feel happy with those activities that cause eventual pain. We can rejoice in doing what is wholesome, and when are doing what is unwholesome, there is no reason for being happy. We also do not need to feel happy about frivolous amusement.

Some individuals feel that laziness is mainly the first kind of laziness of not wanting to practice. Others feel that laziness is the second kind of laziness of being attracted to the unwholesome. A third kind of laziness is simply not having any confidence in ourselves by thinking that we cannot possible accomplish anything as a Buddhist practitioner, and certainly don't have what it takes to become a bodhisattva, much less a Buddha. Having this view is a kind of laziness because the Buddha explained in the Mahayana that even the tiniest insect can attain enlightenment if it has diligence because all sentient beings possess Buddha-nature. So there is no need for us to feel that we as human beings are not capable of attaining enlightenment. When we practice the four preliminaries, the antidote for the lack of wanting to practice is contemplating impermanence and death. The antidote to the laziness of feeling inadequate is contemplating the rarity and difficulty of obtaining a precious human body. When we do this, we will see that since we have been born in a human body and we since have received the Buddhist teachings; we will attain awakening or enlightenment. We might think in a time of desperation, "I do not really dare engage in the activity of a bodhisattva because if I do so I may have to pray all the time, give away everything and even give up my body." This, however, is not well reasoned out because up until now we have undergone vast mountains of suffering in all six realms of existence. We have been beaten, killed, stabbed, and tormented in all possible ways and this has never come to an end. But if we are willing to undergo a small amount of hardship of practicing the dharma, then out difficulty will have had an important purpose—that of permanently ending out suffering. So we should accept a little bit of suffering for the sake of enlightenment.

23. *All physicians bring about health by means of painful treatments; therefore,*
    to destroy many sorrows, a trifle is to be borne:
24. *But the best physician is not one who has given even this suitable treatment.*
    By means of kindly practice he would cure those who are very ill.
25. *At the beginning the Lord compels only the alms of vegetables and such.*

Afterwards he gradually forms one who will sacrifice even his own flesh.

26. *If the knowledge arises that even one's own flesh is as vegetable matter, then what is really difficult about the sacrifice of your flesh and bone?*

27. *One is not unhappy because of the abandonment of misery, he is not melancholy because of learning; since pain is in the mind by false imagining, and in the body because of evil.*

28. *The body is happy by means of merit; the mind is happy by means of learning: What can hurt the Compassionate One as he remains in the realm of rebirth for the sake of others?*

29. *By the power of the awakening mind, one destroys former sins, receives oceans of merit, and is swifter than the shravaka.*

30. *Having obtained the chariot of the awakening mind, which removes all depression and fatigue, going from happiness to happiness, who that is intelligent would be despondent?*

31. *For achieving the welfare of beings, there is the power of zeal, constancy, joy, and release. Eagerness is derived from a fear of sorrow, and it becomes beneficial because of action.*

For instance, if we are ill, the doctor may want to do an operation which will be very painful. But the operation may end the suffering of our illness. In the same way, we should go though the suffering of spiritual practice of the path, to get rid of the suffering of samsara.

Actually, the Buddha has given us very gentle methods for training in enlightenment. The Buddha said that if we are not extremely generous, we can begin by just giving away small things that won't cause us much feeling of loss such as giving away vegetables. Then later on, when the feeling of compassion is really developed, we will not feel any difficulty in giving away something much more difficult such as giving away out own body. Then when we have become a truly great bodhisattva there will be no suffering, no pain because the feeling of pain is the result of doing something unwholesome. When a bodhisattva has abandoned all negative activities there is no suffering of mind or suffering of body because he or she no longer has any attachment to the body. This nonattachment to the body comes from the realization of emptiness and the illusory nature of all things. With the complete realization of emptiness, the bodhisattva will not have any attachment to the body and then will be able to be completely generous and will not feel any suffering.[17]

Due to the strength of awakening mind, the bodhisattva consumes all his previous misdeeds and harbors oceans of merit. The bodhisattva exhausts negative deeds and gathers oceans of merit. Because of this superior aspiration and because if his vast accumulation of merit, the bodhisattva is said to be superior to even the shravakas. So the bodhisattva mounts the horse of awakening mind with the phrase "mounting the horse" with this referring to the fact that once a horse is mounted it is an extremely swift, free and easy way to travel. One can move freely without any weariness of body or mind. Here the awakening mind is likened to a horse and when one mounts awakening mind with its great compassion and understanding of the true nature of phenomena, it is like riding a great horse that proceed swiftly to its goal. One rides this horse of awakening mind going from one joy to the next. So who could ever lapse into despondency?

When traversing the path to enlightenment one should actually take four horses each of which is like a different unit in the army. These units are aspiration, steadfastness, joy, and relaxation. Aspiration is having the strong wish to help all sentient being reach enlightenment, that is freeing everyone from suffering. This strong aspiration needs to be stable, so one never thinks, "I cannot do this." or "I am not suitable to that." One needs to have firm courage that doesn't wane. The second horse is selflessness in which we engage in great joy in whatever we are doing. We should think that helping others towards enlightenment is a wonderful job to be engaged in and in this way proceed joyfully. The third horse is the joy that comes from the other two horses. The fourth horse is relaxation or rest and this means that when one has completed one task, one simply goes on to the next and thus begins new deeds by leaving the completed ones behind. This is like when one has perfected the perfection of generosity, one should proceed on to the perfection of discipline. So these four horses are actually supports for the bodhisattva's activity with the first support, aspiration, being the root of the other three. Without aspiration there will be no selflessness and without this there will be no joy and finally without these two there will be traversing from one level to the next.

We begin to develop the first of these, aspiration, by contemplating the viciousness of samsara and realizing how this cyclic existence causes all our misery. Also by contemplating the benefits of Buddhist practice, the benefits of training as a bodhisattva, and all the benefits arising from enlightened mind will also give rise to aspiration.

32. Then, after having eradicated the enemy, one should strive for an increase of strength, by means of the power of zeal, pride, joy, sacrifice, dedication, and mastery.

33. I am to destroy immeasurable hatreds, both of myself and of others, and in this task the waning of a single "hate" requires oceans of eons.

34. In beginning the waning of hatred, however, the smallest particle [of strength] is not to be observed in me. Destined to immeasurable pain, why does my breast not burst?

35. Many are the virtues, both of myself and of others, which are to be acquired; yet the adding of a single virtue will not occur until after oceans of eons.

36. Never has any increase in virtue arisen in me even the least virtue. How this birth, so marvelously acquired, was uselessly obtained by me!

We need diligence when training in any of the paramitas. When training in generosity, we need diligence, when training in discipline, we need diligence, to develop knowledge and wisdom, we also need diligence. Just as there are different units in an army to carry on a war, so we need the units of aspiration, steadfastness, joy and rest to develop diligence. In addition to these four, there are two more—emphasis and gaining mastery—which are need to develop full diligence.

1. Developing Aspiration

Previously, it was said that the most important quality to develop diligence is aspiration. With aspiration the other qualities come one by one. Since we have been ignorant since beginningless time, we have accumulated an inconceivable number of faults. Not only do we possess a great number of faults and obscurations, but all those around us also have an inconceivable number of faults and obscurations. The person who has promised to clear away all these obscurations is us. We have taken the bodhisattva vow that has promised to clear away all these misfortunes. When we look a little further, we can see that we have to strive and practice hard for eons in order to exhaust even a single one of these faults. So when we consider the magnitude of our task, we then see the need for an incredible amount of diligence to accomplish our aim.

If we discover that we are not actually putting much effort into this project, it is quite embarrassing and painful. Also when we consider the good qualities that we need to develop and the inconceivable number of good qualities that we have promised to foster in each and every sentient being, it can be very discouraging. But then when we look, we see that we are not putting much effort into this project either but we have achieved a precious human birth. It is by some strange coincidence that we have ended up in this situation and if we were truly diligence, we could attain this great goal of Buddhahood. And if we are not diligent, it is a great shame because we will allow this precious human birth just go to waste.

Having entered into the dharma we can make this human birth meaningful by making offerings to the Buddha and those enlightened ones who have entered the world for the welfare of others. We also should try to bring happiness to all sentient beings and when we think about it, this involves giving them the teachings of the Buddha so that they can begin to practice along the path. To do this we need to take care that the teachings of the Buddha do not degenerate and that they develop and expand. In addition to the dharma, we need also to help those who are poor and destitute by giving them clothes, food, and so forth. Helping them make life meaningful is also to give them the gift of fearlessness so that they are not afraid of the many frightening things in life.

To engender diligence we should think of all the things that should be done in order to make a human life have a purpose and that we have not been able to do.

37. *I have not experienced the happiness of great festivals for the worship of the Blessed One. The teaching has not been praised, nor have the poor been satisfied.*

38. *Security has not been given to the fearful, happiness has not been granted to the afflicted. As an arrow from the womb of my mother I have merely shot to sorrow.*

If we are able to achieve a small portion of these things, then there will have been some purpose to being born as a human being. But if we see that we are not accomplishing anything except for giving our mother pain for our birth, then we haven't accomplished anything in this lifetime. When we think along this line, we will feel a sadness and dissatisfaction which will help us develop diligence, the aspiration to develop dharma practice.

How is it that we have ended up in a situation where we have not been accomplishing anything good for ourselves or others. It is because we have not had any interest in the dharma or aspiration to practice in the past. How do we give rise to authentic aspiration? This was answered by the Buddha how said that aspiration is the root of every virtue which comes from being aware of how happiness follows wholesome deeds and how unhappiness follows unwholesome attitudes and deeds. We must become aware of this ripening of karma, the law of cause and effect. If we understand karma, then we will want to engage in the dharma. In the four ordinary foundations[18] we contemplate having a precious human birth, impermanence, the effects of karma, and the drawbacks of samsara to develop aspiration.

Sometimes we will feel physical pain, sometimes unhappiness, or we will feel that what we wish for will not happen. These things come about due to having negative thoughts in the past, from falling under the influence of disturbing emotions or having done negative actions physically. And as a natural ripening of these occurs, we will experience happiness and the fulfillment of their wishes because they have accumulated merit, had a pure attitude, had an authentic good heart, and did good deeds which produces the roots of virtue. This extends on so that virtuous activity ultimately results in going to the pure Buddha realms and enjoying happiness there and receiving the pure *sambhogakaya* teachings of the Buddha. Unvirtuous activity in contrast results in the severe pain and suffering of the hell realms. So understanding how important it is to develop wholesome mental and physical behavior and to avoid as much as possible to fall under the influence of disturbing emotions will create a strong aspiration for the dharma.

39. My birth is such a misfortune now because I previously lacked zeal for the Dharma. Who can reject zeal for the Dharma [without evil consequence]?

40. The Sage has said that zeal is the root of all goodness; and that its root is constant meditation on the maturation of the fruit [of action].

41. For those engaged in evil there arises frustration of desire, and various sorrows, melancholies, and fears.

42. For the doer of good, no matter where his heart's desire turns, there, because of his merits, he is revered as a consequence of the value of the fruit [of his action];

43. but wherever turns the desire of the evildoer for happiness, there, because of his evils, he is smitten with swords of sorrow.

44. Having entered the wide, sweet-smelling, cool womb of the Lotus; having fed upon the kindly words of the Conqueror; having issued in hue beauty from the Enlightenment Lotus created by the Sage those who prosper and advance as a result of their good works, appear as Buddha sons before the Buddha.

45. But howling with suffering the whole skin removed by the demons of Death poured into liquid copper, heated in the fire fragments of flesh cut off by hundreds of blows from burning swords and spear some falls, be cause of evil works, again and again upon the beds of well-heated iron.

46. It follows that one should have zeal for goodness; that one should practice it with ardor; and that having begun the rule of the Vajradhvaja ["He who has the vajra as his banner"], one should have pride.

47. First, all conditions are to be considered. One should begin or not begin, for indeed, not beginning is better than having begun and turning back;

48. *because in another birth this is repeated, and sorrow increases because of evil; and the time for other work is wasted and nothing is accomplished.*
49. *Pride is to be employed in three ways: in work, in opposition to disturbing emotion, and in power. The pride of work is in this knowledge: All is to be done by myself alone.*
50. *This world, self-bound by passion, is not competent for the accomplishment of its own welfare. Therefore I am to do this, since, unlike [most of] mankind, I am not powerless.*
51. *How can I allow another to do a base task while I stand present? If out of pride I do not do it, let pride perish; it is better for me.*

2. Developing Self-confidence

The second unit in the army or the second point is developing self-confidence which sometimes is translated as "pride." we are speaking about not the kind of pride that is a disturbing emotion such as thinking, "I am great" or "I am the best." Rather it is the thought, "I can do it, I am able to accomplish this." This kind of courageous self-confidence is the kind we should develop and is mentioned in the sutra requested by Vajravajya. Before seeing out to do something, we need o see if it is an action that is suitable for us. If we begin it, then we should take care to bring it to completion because a pattern of beginning things and not completing them will just result in our accumulating more suffering.

To take care that we don't start a project that will be left unfinished, we need to have the self-confidence that we can do it. We need the confidence to carry something to completion and this is the power of self-confidence.

If we come under the influence of the disturbing emotions, it will not be possible to help ourselves or others. Falling under the power of disturbing emotions results in our suffering more and to stay clear of these emotions takes diligence. When comparing ourselves with others, we also need to be diligent by seeing how much effort and hardship people are going through to achieve very small pleasures. We should see that to achieve our vast purpose we will have to be just that much more diligent.

52. *Encountering a dead lizard, even the crow is a Garuda. The slightest misfortune oppresses me if my mind is weak.*
53. *When one is made powerless by lassitude, injury easily occurs; but the one who is alert, active, and proud is invincible to the greatest foe.*

So, the self-confidence of action is thinking, "I am able to do this" and the self-confidence of ability is not feeling inadequate, but entering into the activity in a diligent way. This is explained in verse if we encounter a snake that is alive, then even very large birds will have hesitation to attack it. But if the snake is dead, then no one will be afraid—even crows will descend on it. This is because they know that the snake has no power left. The meaning of this example is that we should not be faint-hearted or fall under the weakness of the disturbing emotions. Instead we need to be aware of our actual ability and not fall under the influence of disturbing emotions.

54. *With resolute mind, therefore, I will injure that which is injurious. If I desire the conquest of the three worlds, is it not laughable that calamity conquer me?*
55. *All is to be conquered by me, I am not to be conquered by anyone this is the pride which I shall bear, for I am a son of the Conqueror Lion.*

With self-confidence and courage that we feel with "I can actually do this" and with the knowledge of our actual capacity to do something results in a steadiness or steadfastness. If we have great self-confidence, then even the greatest obstacle will not stop us, but if we do not have self-confidence, then even the smallest obstacle will prevent us from doing what we want to do. So to not overcome our feelings of inadequacy will result in our desire to liberate all the beings of the three realms become just a joke. So we must be confident and it was said that the Buddha was like a lion who was able to accomplish everything that needed to be accomplished without a change of their being an obstacle. In the same way we must have the same courage know that as a bodhisattva we will be able to attain anything that we wish to attain.

56. *Whatever beings have been conquered by pride are miserable, they are not the proud ones: Proud persons are not submissive to the enemy, but they are submissive to the enemy who is pride.*
57. *They have been brought by arrogance to misfortune; even in the human condition their joys are lost. Eating the ritual rice balls of others: slaves, stupid, ugly, weak,*
58. *despised on all sides, stiffened by arrogance; these are the wretched ones. If they are among the proud, then tell me what kind are miserable?*
59. *Those are truly proud, victorious, and even heroic, who destroy pride for the conquering of the enemy, pride; who having destroyed that struggling and treacherous pride, gladly bestow the fruit of victory upon mankind.*

There are two kinds of pride: one based on disturbing emotions which results in suffering and the pride of thinking one will be able to overcome the disturbing emotions, fulfill the activity of the bodhisattvas which is very conducive to practice. The text says if we find ourselves in the midst of disturbing emotions, we must by all means take care not to fall under the influence of them. In the same way that a lion that is surrounded by jackals will remain fearless and unharmed because the jackals will have any chance to harm the lion.

60. *In the midst of a multitude of disturbing emotions one should be a thousand times more fierce and as hard to be conquered by the hosts of passion as the lion by herds of antelopes.*

61. *Since even in the most painful situation the eye cannot behold the essence of it, so likewise when one is caught in a painful situation he must not be obedient to passion.*

Just as when people are doing a job decide to put it aside because they feel too cold, hungry, or uncomfortable and think, "I'll get back to it later." But if there is a danger of them losing their eyesight because they don't get the job done, they will give the job top priority and not give it up when they become hungry or cold. Similarly, being burned will cause suffering, but it is not a great suffering compared to the suffering encountered when one falls under the influence of disturbing emotions.

Also if one is burned, one will suffer and die. If on the other hand you compare that to falling under the influence of disturbing emotions, then also it is better to be burnt. Also if one has one's head cut off, it is very painful, but when compared to the power of falling under disturbing emotions, this is not a great concern.

3. Working with Great Joy

62. *The one who rushes to an activity will be one who is too fond of that activity, insatiable in devotion to that activity, like one striving to win the joy of a prize in sport.*

63. *How can such a one whose happiness is activity be happy when not active; since, whether or not there is happiness in it, he engages in activity for the sake of happiness?*

64. *It is because of desire, which is like honey on a razor's edge, that there is no satisfaction in the realms of rebirth. Because of the death of merit, how can there exist the satisfaction which is the result of a sweet and auspicious ripening of merit?*

Thirdly, everything must be done out of great joy. As it says in verse 62,

"Just like those who yearn for the fruits of play," meaning just like small children who are having a very good time playing will not feel hungry or tired. Because they enjoy what they do, the bodhisattva similarly is greatly delighted to help others and does whatever he or she does with a great joy permeating it all, never feeling weary or feeling tired in any way.

We need to have happiness in doing whatever we do so we never feel like we've had enough. We always just wish for more because it is really enjoyable. Ordinary persons put a lot of effort into acquiring sensual enjoyment and pleasures and no matter how much they get, they do not feel satisfied and just with for more. Enjoying sensual pleasures is a bit like licking honey off a razor's edge. The honey itself is sweet and tastes good, but since the razor is sharp, liking the honey becomes painful. Although the effects of striving for sensual enjoyment is painful, they never feel satisfied. But a bodhisattva, for whom the result of the action is joy and happiness, every action is happiness and enjoyable.

4. Abandonment

65. *Furthermore, at the conclusion of an activity, does one plunge again into action like an elephant, overheated at midday and finding lakes, plunges into the first one [he encounters]?*

66. *Rather, when one has endured to the end of his strength, he should retire in order to act again; and having accomplished much, he should rest from activity because of [the danger of] ever increasing thirst.*

67. *He must guard completely against the blows of passion, and firmly strike back, like a man who enters a sword fight against a clever enemy.*

68. *When one becomes fearful, he ought to seize his discarded sword; and so also, remembering hell, one should seize the lost sword of mindfulness).*

69. *Poison, when it reaches the bloodstream, pervades the body, and likewise aversion, having found an opening, pervades the mind.*

70. *Like the bearer of a vessel of off, who standing in the midst of naked swords fears death if he stumbles, so is the one who has taken the [Bodhisattva] vow.*

71. *Just as one immediately leaps up when a snake is in his lap, he quickly should resist the approach of sleep and of slothfulness.*

72. *In the case of every single fault, having done suitable austerity, he should reflect, "What shall I do that I may not do this again?"*

73. *For this cause he will wish to obtain proper companions and activity, thinking, "In what circumstances may the practice of mindfulness exist?"*

74. *As he ought to make ready the self, remembering the Speech on Heedfulness (apramada); so at the approach of action, before its coming, he turns in every direction.*

75. *As cotton is obedient to the coming and going of the wind, so one should proceed in obedience to his resolution; and thus power riddhi) is completely triumphant.*

Verse 74 says we should leave everything that we are doing, in order to return to it later. This means that if we come to a point where we think that now we are actually unable to continue with this, we should decide to take a break. For example, if we do the preliminaries with a lot of prostrations, we can develop pain in the knees and then if we just go on doing prostrations, it would not be so good in the long run. Instead it is better to take a break and let the knees heal and continue when we are capable of prostrations. Also having done something well, we should put it aside with a desire to accomplish what will follow. This is the second aspect of giving up, one of the four units. Having reached the end of a particular stage of the path, we should not think, "Oh, I'll just keep going on with this" but instead go on to the next step and apply ourselves diligently to that step. That also comes under "giving up," or abandonment.

In addition to the four units, there are the two powers, of which the first is mindfulness which concentrates on diligence. Just as a warrior, when going to the battlefield, will need to be very mindful, taking care not to be killed by the enemy. He needs to take care that he can definitely stab the enemy. In the same way, to accomplish prostrations we need carefulness and mindfulness.

We need mindfulness in the same way as we have it if we are engage in a fight. If we suddenly see that we have lost our knife in a battle, we need to get it back immediately. In the same way, when practicing if we discover that we are losing mindfulness, be need to quickly recall the unfortunate effects of lax practice and the fearful experiences we can undergo in the hell realms. We should immediately regain our mindfulness.

We need to be very disciplined and take care to do only what is really appropriate and suitable. Just as if we were carrying a jar full to the brim with oil and someone says if a single drop spills from this jar, we will be killed, we should take very good care to do what is right and appropriate in this situation. Similarly, when practicing, we need to be constantly aware of not falling under the power of disturbing emotions.

We need also to act immediately in our training. Just as a coward who discovers a poisonous snake in his lap will immediately jump up; in the same way, when we discover we are becoming sleepy, getting dull, we should immediately think, "I am not going to achieve what I set out to do" and be diligent.

The second of the two powers is to gain mastery. Before doing something I should recall before taking any action and do it joyfully. Gaining mastery means we should immediately, without any kind of delay, engage in what is to be done. We should not think, "I'll do it later," or "I'll just do it tomorrow." But we should do it immediately, "Just as the wind blows a piece of cotton, just so I will be controlled by joy."

In this way accomplish everything. Just as a piece of cotton has no power to stay in one place when wind blows, going to the west if the wind blows west, going east if the wind blows east. In the same way, we should be controlled by joy and out of this great joy, accomplish everything.

A Brief Biography of Thrangu Rinpoche

Thrangu Rinpoche was born in Kham in 1933. At the age of five he was formally recognized by the Sixteenth Karmapa and the previous Situ Rinpoche as the incarnation of the great Thrangu tulku. Entering Thrangu monastery, from the ages of seven to sixteen he studied reading, writing, grammar, poetry, and astrology, memorized ritual texts, and completed two preliminary retreats. At sixteen under the direction of Khenpo Lodro Rabsel he began the study of the three vehicles of Buddhism while staying in retreat.

At twenty-three he received full ordination from the Karmapa. When he was twenty-seven Rinpoche left Tibet for India at the time of the Chinese military takeover. He was called to Rumtek, Sikkim, where the Karmapa had his seat in exile. At thirty-five he took the geshe examination before 1500 monks at Buxador monastic refugee camp in Bengal, and was awarded the degree of Geshe Lharampa. On his return to Rumtek he was named Abbot of Rumtek monastery and the Nalanda Institute for Higher Buddhist studies at Rumtek. He has been the personal teacher of the four principal Karma Kagyu tulkus: Shamar Rinpoche, Situ Rinpoche, Jamgon Kongtrul Rinpoche and Gyaltsab Rinpoche.

Thrangu Rinpoche has traveled extensively throughout Europe, the Far East and the USA; he is the abbot of Gampo Abbey, Nova Scotia, Canada, of Thrangu House, Oxford, in the UK. In 1984 he spent several months in Tibet where he ordained over 100 monks and nuns and visited several monasteries. He has also founded the monastery, Thrangu Tashi Choling in Bodhnath, a retreat center and college at Namo Buddha, east of the Katmandu Valley, and has established a school in Bodhnath for the general education of lay children and young monks. He built Tara Abbey in Katmandu. In October of 1999 he consecrate the College at Sarnath which will accept students from the different sects of Buddhism and will be available to western students as well.

Thrangu Rinpoche has given teachings in over 25 countries and is especially known for taking complex teachings and making them accessible to Western students. Thrangu Rinpoche is a recognized master of Mahamudra meditation.

More recently, because of his vast knowledge of the Dharma, he was appointed by His Holiness the Dalai Lama to be the personal tutor for the 17th Karmapa.

Chapter 8

The Perfection of Meditation

In the last chapter we discussed how to develop diligence. We need to be diligent to train in developing meditation and wisdom. This is because if we don't apply ourselves to meditation, then we will become distracted. Interestingly, we don't become distracted from doing unwholesome things and start doing wholesome things; rather because of our habituation from beginningless time to what is unwholesome, when we become distracted it is towards the unwholesome caused by the influence of disturbing emotions and negative deeds. In order not to come under the power of disturbing emotions, we need to apply ourselves diligently to the practice of meditation.

1. *Having thus increased one's energy, the mind should be established in meditation (samadhi), since the man of agitated mind stands between the fangs of passion.*
2. *By the isolation of body and mind there is no occasion for being agitated. It follows that having forsaken the world, one should turn his thinking upside down.*
3. *Because of attachment due to a thirst for profits and the like, the world is not forsaken. It follows that the knowing one, when in the act of renunciation, ought so to reflect.*
4. *By means of tranquillity (Shamatha) one achieves clarity of vision (Vipashyana). The tranquil person destroys passion when he has become tranquil. The chief goal of that which merits one's desire is tranquillity; and this comes through indifference to the world.*

What are the circumstances for developing good meditation? One is going on retreat by letting the body remain in solitude. If one is not capable of fully giving up and letting go of wealth, possessions, and clothing then one must begin by not having attachment to these things. Not being too tied up with material things also is a form of solitude. Having a mind remaining in solitude is to give up conceptual thinking because one sees it as faulty and mistaken. When one relies on these two types of solitude, then it is possible for a very special kind of meditation.

To give up worldly life can cause obstacles. There are two kinds of factors for making it impossible for oneself to give up worldly life? One is the inner attachment of being attached to friends and relatives, father, mother, children. To have this kind of attachment to other sentient beings makes it impossible for oneself to apply oneself fully to practice of dharma. Then there is the outer attachment of the craving for wealth, possessions, good food, and clothes, and certain enjoyments. This kind of craving, this dependency as outer possessions and temporary enjoyments, makes it impossible for us to feel the courage which is needed for dharma practice. Outer possessions and enjoyments also function as obstacles for us to have the actual power to engage ourselves in dharma practice. So we need to rid ourselves of both these concerns.

So we train in meditation. We may also feel, "I'm training in meditation but there is not really any development taking place. I'm not progressing much." This occurs because the clear seeing aspect (Vipashyana) of meditation is introduced too early so that the qualities of meditation cannot really unfold. In the fourth verse "by superior insight completely endowed with calm abiding" This means that success in meditation practice comes about when there is real true stability in calm abiding (Shamatha) meditation. When Shamatha practice has become really well developed, then the wisdom of Vipashyana can arise and the disturbing emotions can be overcome. When disturbing emotions are overcome, then true realization can unfold. This is an important point. For true meditation practice to take place, we need the full ability in Shamatha practice. So whether we have been introduced to he wisdom of Vipashyana or not, first we need to extensively practice Shamatha.

There was a meditation place with a great master, and the students, the meditation practitioners who came from this place to practice would all have very great experience and insight. So many great practitioners came from this place because the meditation master would not introduce the knowledge of Vipashyana until the disciples had trained in the four preliminary practices. They needed to carry out 400,000 prostrations, recite the mantra of vajrasattva 400,000 times offer 400,000 mandalas, and train the guru yoga 400,000 times. Only after having purified and gathered aspirations of the preliminaries, after having developed strong confidence and devotion, would they be introduced to Vipashyana. This introduction to Vipashyana happened naturally with this strong foundation in Shamatha. For this reason, we need to take care to become very stable in our dharma practice, to develop much devotion and sincere interest, so that Vipashyana can be introduced and the good qualities of practice can unfold. In this text it says how it is important to develop strength of calm abiding. How is it possible to reach tranquillity meditation. It comes about when we are unattached to worldly affairs. By being unattached to worldly life, we enjoy great happiness and then Shamatha meditation happens.

5. *Who among transient creatures merits the attachment of a transient creature? He will not see the loved one again for thousands of births.*

6. *Not seeing [the beloved], one walks without joy, and he is not established in meditation (samadhi); and yet, having seen the beloved, one is not satisfied and one's thirst is tormented as before.*

7. *One does not see things as they are; he is left behind because of emotional tumult; he burns with that grief which is caused by desire for union with the dear one.*

8. *Because of this foolish thinking, life passes quickly again and again. Because of a transient companion, one falls from the eternal Dharma.*

9. *When one moves in the company of fools, he goes inevitably to misery; yet when one is different from them, he is not wanted. What is gained by consorting with fools?*

10. *One moment they are friends; the next they are enemies. They become enraged when circumstances are pleasing. Common men are hard to comprehend.*

11. *When they are advised for their own good, they are enraged and they prevent one from anything useful; yet if one does not listen to them, they are angry and they become miserable.*

12. *Envious of a superior man, hostile to an equal, arrogant to an inferior, infatuated by praise, and angered by blame: What good can come from a fool?*

13. *Boastful of self, blaming others, conversant with the pleasures of rebirth, something of the fool's evil comes inevitably from one fool to another.*

14. *In this way, through the association of one fool with another, there is an encountering of the unwholesome. I shall dwell alone, happy and undisturbed in mind.*

15. *One should flee far from the fool. When one meets him, one should conciliate him with amenities; yet not in order to be bound in intimacy; rather, like a holy man, one is indifferent.*

16. *After taking only that which is required for the sake of the Dharma, like the bee taking honey from the flower, I shall dwell everywhere, unknown, like the new moon.*

There are two factors to make us attracted towards worldly life. One is the inner attachment of being attached to our father, mother, friends, and relatives. The other is the outer craving for possessions, wealth, and enjoyment. First of all, it explains how being attached to sentient beings is an obstacle to dharma practice. Having other sentient beings depending on us will prevent much success in our dharma practice. So in verse five it says we are impermanent and other sentient beings are also impermanent. So when impermanence is attracted to impermanence, there is nothing gained in such a relationship. If we were impermanent and the other were permanent, then we could help the other. If both were permanent, then also there would be an effect happening. But since we are impermanent, and other sentient beings are impermanent, there is absolutely nothing to place our trust in, in this kind of relationship.

So here we may get a little confused, thinking isn't the dharma about helping sentient beings, yet here it says we are to stay away from sentient beings. How could this be? This comes about because we are talking in this case about relating to sentient beings with desire and attachment, with our own need to relate to sentient beings due to a need that we have. When we relate to sentient beings, because we crave the company of sentient beings, there can be no positive effect. We will not be able to help ourselves, much less other sentient beings. We can actually help other sentient beings by practicing true compassion. But when the relationship is based on craving and need, then nothing can be accomplished. So by thinking only of desire, this life will pass without any meaning. Friends and relatives will even destroy the meaning I need these friends of mine. When we have an attitude based on desire, then we will not be able to practice the dharma whole-heartedly. Not only that, but by putting so much energy into socializing with other sentient beings, we will destroy the capability of benefiting sentient beings, namely, the dharma that reaches permanent liberation.

15. *One should flee far from the fool. When one meets him, one should conciliate him with amenities; yet not in order to be bound in intimacy; rather, like a holy man, one is indifferent.*

16. *After taking only that which is required for the sake of the Dharma, like the bee taking honey from the flower, I shall dwell everywhere, unknown, like the new moon.*

17. *Many, like myself, desire profit and honor, but when seized by death, the fear of death arises.*

18. *Whatever the mind infatuated with pleasure finds to be a joy, that very thing, having become sorrow, stands multiplied a thousand times.*

19. *Thus wisdom may not seek [pleasure], because danger results from desire: but if [pleasure] comes by itself, after having made fast [the mind], let one behold it.*

20. *Many have become rich, and many famous; but they have not known where they go with wealth and fame.*

21. *Some despise me: But why do I rejoice when praised? Some praise me: But*

why am I depressed when censured?
22. *Beings are of diverse propensities and they are not satisfied even by the*
  Conquerors (jina). How, then, by an ignorant person like myself? How,
  then, by thinking of the world

How should we relate to sentient beings when we meet them? This is explained in verse 15 which says one should remain far from sentient beings, but when we encounter them; we should maintain a pleasing countenance, smiling and behaving politely, and behave as if we are happy to meet them. On the other hand, we should also not act as a real close friend with a special relationship. Because if we do this, then this will produce anger or desire later on. So appearing to be happy to meet with others, but not associating very closely with whomever we meet is how we should act.

By thinking of attachment to wealth and possessions should make us terrified after death is presented in verse 17. We should not put much effort into accumulating honor and praise and also not put too much effort into accumulating material wealth. If we happen to be in a situation where people are praising us and where we are enjoying good material circumstances, and if we become proud of this thinking, "I'm very special and very popular and rich." we must realize that this kind of self-importance can only produce suffering later on. Whatever we are attached to, that attachment will become the cause of suffering many times greater than the original attachment was in the future. It says here "Whenever one has attachment to something, then that attachment will become the cause of many fold suffering in the future."

It is also possible to be attached to the occasion when someone praises us and we feel happy and crave such situations. Then when people criticize us, we begin to feel angry. But when looking at the situation a little further, we see there is actually no real reason why we should feel happy when people praise us and upset when people put us down. When we are praised, others are feeling put down; when we are criticized, others are feeling better than us. So why should we become happy when praised and depressed when criticized because the opposite is going on with others.

23. *Beings despise the poor; they think ill of the rich. How can pleasure arise*
  from those who by nature dwell together in sorrow?
24. *It has been said by the Buddhas that the fool is the friend of no one, because*
  no pleasure arises within the fool except with regard to self-interest.
25. *Whatever pleasure is related to one's own interest is only the pleasure of*

self-interest. Likewise, anger, as when one has lost money, is only caused by a loss of pleasure.

26. *Trees do not think ill nor are they to be excessively honored. When may I dwell with such pleasant companions!*

27. *When may I walk with indifference, never looking be hind, staying in an empty temple, in a thicket of trees, or in caves?*

28. *When shall I dwell without a resting place, following my own inclinations, in broad natural places without attachments?*

29. *When shall I dwell without fear, without protecting the body; the measure of my property, a clay bowl; my robe worthless to thieves?*

30. *When shall I compare my body, the bearer of decay, with other skeletons, after going to my own cemetery?*

31. *This body of mine will become so putrid that even jackals will not be able to prowl near to it because of its stench.*

32. *The fragments of bone which naturally belong to the body and are a part of its unity, disintegrate one by one. How much more another beloved person!*

33. *Man is born alone, and alone he dies. None other has a share in his suffering. What use are friends? What use are obstacle makers?*

34. *As one who has begun a journey is accepted as a guest in a dwelling, so the traveler through life is accepted as a guest in the dwelling of birth.*

When we go through this kind of reasoning, it becomes much easier to give up attachment. When we are not attached, then good qualities in us will unfold unhindered. When we are not attached, we will be able to remain in solitude which is conducive to meditation. So the next verses praise the good qualities of a solitary retreat by saying, "When one goes to live alone in the forest and relies upon oneself independently, then the trees and birds will also be there." But these animals don't tell you that you are no good or that they don't like you. They won't do anything to disturb you. So when you remain in their company, they will be perfect company and there will be no obstacles to your dharma practice. Instead you will enjoy developing good qualities.

In a solitary retreat, when we are dwelling in a place that does not belong to anyone else, it will be joyful. If we can stay there without holding on to it mentally, then it will be an extremely enjoyable experience and we can have a relaxed and open mind making everything conducive for practice. There will be no obstacle to living according to the dharma and for this reason we need to rely upon solitary places.

35. *Let one proceed to the forest, without grieving on the part of relatives, before he is taken there anyway by the four corpse bearers;*

36. *without friendship without hindrance without fear his body solitary and insignificant, he does not grieve at dying, because already he has died to*

the world

37. and he will not be in the vicinity of any intruder whose grieving causes pain. Not one of them can disturb his recollection of the Buddha.

Verse 35 begins a discussion of when one dies. If we can live without attachment, living in contentment and joy in solitary places, then there will be only circumstances that are good for dharma practice with few obstacles. If we are already "counted as a dead man" meaning that we have said good-bye to, the world when we die will have no mourner around our deathbed. Even if there were one hundred people standing at our deathbed, they would be unable to help relive us of any of the pain of dying and they would, obviously, not be able to accompany us where we are going. Furthermore, a group of relatives around our deathbed may even distract us from supplicating the Buddha, the dharma, and the sangha. Our mourners could distract our mind at this critical time and so this is not good and it is better to rely on a solitary retreat.

The text then explains how to abandon worldly life, how to live without much material comfort, how to become independent of worldly life. This is to live in contentment in retreat without requiring much material comfort and is very conducive to training in meditation. Next we must pacify conceptual mind and develop a gentle and peaceful frame of mind.

38. It follows that solitude are pleasing, kindly, the dawn of all that is auspicious, the tranquilizers of all disturbance. Let me always frequent them.

39. Liberated from the thought of anything else, the mind centered one-pointedly upon its own thought, I shall strive for the composing of thought and its control.

40. Desires indeed are the progenitors of ill fortune, both here in this world and elsewhere. Here: by means of bondage, murder, and mutilation. Elsewhere: in hell and the like.

41. Whatever [you desired] for the sake of which prayer was made many times to go betweens and procurers, for the sake of which neither evil nor disgrace was ever counted,

42. and which cast the self into fear, and which wasted wealth; whatever you have embraced, which appeared to be the uttermost beatitude,

43. is none other than bones. They are at your own disposal and without perception. Having embraced them with delight, how is it that you do not go to beatitude?

44. That face which was covered by a veil whether it was seen or unseen, which was raised up only with effort, and bent down because of modesty;

45. *that face is now exposed by vultures as if they cannot bear your discomfort. Behold it! Why do you run from it?*
46. *It was this which was protected from even the glance of another's eye that now is devoured. Why do you not jealously protect it?*
47. *After you have seen this mountain of flesh devoured by vultures and other scavengers, you do not honor their food with garlands, sandal, and ornaments?*
48. *You are terrified by the sight of this motionless skeleton. Why are you not also afraid of it when it is moved by some demon?*
49. *Saliva and excrement are born from the same source from food! Since excrement is unpleasant to you, how can the drinking of saliva [in a kiss] be so precious?*
50. *Those who love have intercourse with mere pillows that are filled with cotton and soft to the touch. Thinking that their emission is not a stench, they are infatuated with excrement.*

To develop a peaceful mind that is not under the influence of disturbing emotions, we need to have little desire and to eliminate craving. This is because most of the suffering that we will go thorough in this life, comes from craving or desire. If we are put in prison, if we are beaten up, most likely this is caused by our craving. So in this life countless difficulties and pain which we undergo is caused by desire. In the next lifetime, this desire is also what sends us into the hell realms. So by contemplating the amount of pain in this life, and the even greater pain in the next lifetime that comes about because of desire, we should try to eliminate our desire.

The Attachment to Disturbing Emotions

51. *When it is covered, even this [body] is an object of passion. Why is it not loved when it is uncovered? If the covering is not the object, why is it caressed?*
52. *If these two impurities [of bone and of flesh] are not objects of passion for you, why embrace again a cage of bones fastened with sinews and completely smeared with the filth of flesh?*
53. *By means of your own great excrement be content. You who are ravenous for feces, forget that other pouch of excrement!*
54. *"I love that flesh," you say. You desire to see and to touch. How can you want flesh when by its nature it is without thought?*
55. *That though which you seek, you are not able to see or to touch; and that which you can touch and see does not realize it. Why then do you embrace in vain?*
56. *It is no wonder that you do not realize the body of another to be excrement; but that you do not perceive your own body to be excrement is amazing.*

57. *After having renounced the young lotus, radiant with the rays of the sun in a cloudless sky, what joy is there to the mind to be drunk with excrement in a cage of feces?*

58. *If you do not wish to touch the earth, and so forth, because it is smeared with excrement, how can you wish to touch that body from which the refuse is cast out?*

59. *If you do not have a passion for these two impurities [the body and its refuse], why do you embrace another who is born from a field of excrement, its seed and that by which it grows?*

60. *You do not desire the filthy worm which is produced from excrement, because of its minuteness: But you seek that great excrement the body born of excrement!*

61. *Not only do you not detest your own excrement, O ravenous for feces! You desire other vessels of excrement!*

62. *When dainty foods, the seasoning of boiled rice, camphor, and so forth, are thrown from the mouth and spit out, even the earth becomes impure.*

63. *If you do not admit the excrement [of your own body] although it is before your eyes, then observe the horrible bodies of others who have been thrown into a cemetery.*

64. *When the skin splits open great fear arises as a consequence. How indeed can joy ever arise again after one has known what it is like to be in that place?*

65. *The perfume which pervades the body [of the corpse] is from sandalwood and not from anything else. Why are you attracted elsewhere because of the perfume belonging to another?*

66. *If your foul-smelling person is not an object of passion, is that not indeed propitious? Why does the world, longing for that which is contrary to its welfare, anoint it with perfume?*

67. *What then has happened to the body if its pleasant smell is sandalwood? Why are you attracted elsewhere because of the perfume belonging to another?*

68. *If the hair and nails are long, the teeth are spotted and yellow, the naked body, covered with dirt, is horrible by nature.*

69. *Why do you adore it zealously, providing a sword for self-destruction? The earth is filled with madmen laboring for self-deception.*

70. *Having seen many skeletons, you find that a cemetery is disgusting to you: But you delight in a village, which is a cemetery filled with walking skeletons.*

71. *And yet even that excrement is not obtained without price: the fatigue of achieving prosperity and the torment which begins in hell.*

The antidote for the disturbing emotions is knowledge or wisdom which is taught in the ninth chapter of this book. An antidote to the disturbing emotion of anger is taught in the chapter on patience. An antidote to the disturbing emotion of desire is taught in this chapter on meditation. Desire expresses itself in two ways: being attached to friends and relatives which prevents us from remaining in a natural peaceful way and craving for outer possessions which prevents us from devoting much time to dharma practice. Generally we need to remain free from the craving of our friends and relatives and especially stay clear of the great attachment of sexual relations.

First a beginner has no consideration for whatever negative consequences of forming attachments and understanding the consequences of such actions. We may have to sacrifice all our wealth for this relationship. If we investigate the actual nature of the object of our desire, we find that the lover is not made up of something valuable or beautiful such as diamonds or gold. Our lover will eventually be nothing but a skeleton. When we look closer it becomes clear that the person that we desire is not anything special. If we got to an Eastern cemetery, we will become afraid of seeing the corpses laying around. But, actually the one we were so interested in (our lover) is nothing other than just this. So why are we not afraid when meeting our lover? This mental training to reduce attachment to others is described in detail in the text.

We need to realize that there is no need to have great craving to mental objects we are attached to because of the difficulties getting to them and by understanding the cost that we pay in order to get them. We go through lots of pain, and we create lots of evil and unwholesomeness in order to get them so there is no reason to be attached to them.

For the sake of that particle of sweetness which is obtained without effort even by the beast, this brief advantage, so hard to obtain, is destroyed by an evil destiny. Inevitably the way of trivialities is through the mountains of hell. Whatever is done for the sake of bodies is always painful.

Attachment to Wealth

72. *The child has not the ability to earn: What pleasure is there in youth? Youthfulness passes in earning. Grown old, what is done for pleasure?*

73. *Some, who have evil desires, are thoroughly worn-out at the day's end because of their occupations: Coming home in the evening they lie down as if they were dead.*

74. *Others, because of military expeditions, are grieved by the anguish of dwelling abroad: For years they do not see the sons and the wives for whom they long.*

75. *Whoever has sold himself for prosperity, because of the infatuation of*

desire, he has not obtained it: But instead, his life has been led vainly in the
service of others.

76 *Their own bodies having been sold, they always are engaged in rendering*
service, while their wives give birth in forest thickets and such places.

77. *They go into battle at the risk of their lives just in order to live. The*
bewildered, distorted by desire, go into slavery for the sake of pride.

78. *Some who are victims of desire are thrown on spikes and pierced; others are*
beheld burning and smitten with swords.

79. *Fortune, because of acquiring, protecting, and despairing of hope, is the*
most endless misfortune. Because of eagerness to cling determinedly to
wealth, one is without opportunity for release from the sorrow of existence.

80. *Such is the misery which abounds for the one who desires, and its sweetness*
is as slight as the particle of food received by a beast who pulls a cart.

81. *For the sake of that particle of sweetness which is obtained without effort*
even by the beast, this brief advantage, so hard to obtain, is destroyed by an
evil destiny. Inevitably the way of trivialities is through the mountains of
hell. Whatever is done for the sake of bodies is always painful.

Verse 72 explains that there is also no reason to be attached to wealth
and possessions. On top of that, there is also great misery connected with
being attached in worldly wealth and possessions. We go through a lot of
trouble in order to collect wealth and then we go through trouble and
difficulty to protect it and take care that no thief will come and to avoid
anything that would destroy it. Then when we are no longer able to
protect it, the wealth is lost. In this way, there is a lot of pain associated
with wealth and possessions. When we put energy to securing
possessions and are attached to wealth, then we are not able to practice
the dharma and reach liberation from suffering and attain happiness.

82. *But Buddhahood is obtained by even a fraction of the effort required in*
hundreds of millions of years in the realms of rebirth. From the course of
sorrow comes great sorrow, and the one involved in desire has neither
Buddhahood nor Enlightenment.

83. *When one remembers the anguish of hell, neither sword nor poison nor fire*
nor precipice nor enemies are equal [in danger] to one's desires.

84. *Consequently, relinquishing desire, let joy arise in tranquil forest places,*
empty of strife and of labor.

Whatever is done out of desire will have unfortunate results. There is a
lot of suffering that comes about due to desire. Enlightenment itself is
reached by just going through a tiny bit of suffering compared to the
amount of suffering that we go thorough as a result of desire. So the
amount of suffering which it takes to enlightenment is very little

compared to what we go through as a result of desire. The suffering that we take upon ourselves to reach enlightenment has a great purpose, whereas, the suffering that comes about because of desire is completely wasted and without any meaning.

The Joys of Solitude

85. *Fortunate are those on delightful rock terraces, broad as palaces, cool as sandal and moonbeam; their minds are fanned by noiseless, delightful forest winds.*

86. *The Bodhisattva comes and goes and thinks on the true welfare of others.*

87. *He wanders wherever and whenever he wishes in secret places, at the foot of a tree, in an empty house freed from the distress of acquiring and of protecting. Without distraction, he walks as he wishes.*

88. *His behavior is according to his own inclination. His dwelling place is limited in no way whatever. He enjoys that contentment and happiness which is rare even to Indra.*

89. *Thus, in such examples, by contemplation of the virtues of solitude, the imagination is pacified and the Awakening mind is cultivated.*

When discussing how to give up worldly life, we will discuss mostly the actual distance between us and wealth and possessions. Giving up material possessions is more here a matter of how to change our attitude, how to purify the mind, and how to create a wholesome attitude.

Generally, we may think that wealth and enjoyment, the sense of pleasure can give us a lot of what we can really enjoy, but actually we don't get that much enjoyment from such pleasures. For example, when I went to Bhutan with His Holiness the Karmapa, we were invited by the king of Bhutan to come and visit his palace. Bhutan is not a very developed country, but the palace of the king of Bhutan was extremely beautiful and furnished all the kinds of comforts. There was a beautiful garden around the palace with extremely beautiful dancers continually doing performances. There were many other pleasures at this palace. My first thought was, "How wonderful, it must be great to live here!" But later when the King requested an interview with the Karmapa, the King began to tell a story that was full of sadness and misfortune. I was quite surprised and shocked to hear how much pain and misery the King of Bhutan was going through. It was a story of misery much worse that any of us normal beings could tell. It was quite an interesting lesson.

So when we think of how it is to live in a solitary retreat, we can see that in retreat we cannot get into a dispute with others and so there is no circumstances to give rise to disturbing emotions and therefore it is a wonderful place to be. Remaining in retreat what great benefits to sentient beings we can carry out. So we should remember how fortunate that it is to enter a solitary retreat with no striving and no disturbing emotions. During this we shall benefit sentient being in a very vast way.

In a solitary retreat we are totally free being under no one's control, not one to disagree with or fight with, nothing that would cause a disturbing emotion to arise. So remaining in a retreat is wonderful. Such an enjoyable situation is very difficult to find anywhere else. Even the god Indra does not enjoy the same kind of happiness that can be found in a solitary retreat.

Giving up worldly life, abandoning contemplation and recalling the qualities of solitary places are all conducive circumstances for actual meditation to take place. When worldly life is renounced, when we have given up attachment to sentient beings, wealth, and enjoyment, and we have gone into a solitary place, then that is the time to engage in actual meditation practice. That is when the actual training in meditation.

5. Exchanging Self for Others

90. *Primarily, one should zealously cultivate the equality of the other and of the self. All joys and sorrows are equal, and I am to guard them like my own.*
91. *The body, by splitting up the hand and so on, has many parts, yet it is to be preserved as one: So likewise the world divided into parts is undivided, since everything is composed of sorrow and of joy.*
92. *If my sorrow does not injure the bodies of others, nonetheless, because of attachment to the self, that sorrow is unbearable to me.*
93. *Likewise, if another's sorrow is unintelligible to me, nonetheless, because of attachment to the self, that sorrow is unbearable to him.*
94. *Another's sorrow is to be destroyed by me because it is sorrow like my own sorrow. Others, also, are to be favored by me because their creaturehood is like my own creaturehood.*
95. *Since a neighbor and I are equal in desiring happiness, what is the unique quality of the "self" which requires an effort for happiness?*
96. *Since both fear and sorrow are neither desirable to my neighbor nor to me, what is the unique quality of that "self" which I protect instead of him?*
97. *Because I am not oppressed by reason of his sorrow, is he not to be protected? Am I not to protect myself from the injury which will come from the sorrow of future bodies?*
98. *Surely it is a false calculation to think that there is an "I," because it is another who has died and it is another who is born.*
99. *So if anyone is protected from any sorrow, it is regarded as his own. The*

sorrow of the foot is not that of the hand, so why is it protected by the hand?

100. *Even if unrelated, it arises from the Egomaker (ahamkara). Whatever is unrelated, both to one's self or to another, is to be annulled with all one's might.*

101. *"Continuity" (samtana) and "aggregate" (samudaya} are like a group or an army or such: They are false. There is no "he" of whom there is sorrow; and because of this, whose will be this "his"?*

102. *All sorrows, without distinction, are ownerless; and because of misery they are to be prevented. Why then is restriction made?*

103. *Why is sorrow to be prevented? All are without disagreement [on this point]. And if it is to be prevented, then [let it be done] completely. Not just in myself. Everywhere!*

104. *If great sorrow is derived from compassion, why allow it to arise against one's will? After considering the sorrow of the world, how great is the sorrow of the compassionate!*

105. *If the sorrow of the many vanishes by the sorrow of the one, then that sorrow ought to arise from pity of one's self and of others.*

When we start out training in bodhichitta we should, first of all, begin training in relative bodhichitta using two methods to do this. One is making ourselves equal to others and the other is exchanging ourselves for others. We have a strong attachment to ourselves; we want to nourish and cherish ourselves and we're not very interested in what happens to others. We have this clinging to ego. To eliminate this we can first train in considering ourselves equal to others. Then based on this training, we can actually be able to change the emphasis so that others become the important ones and we become not so interesting and important. If we go about it in this order, it becomes easier to reach the desired goal.

To develop equality between self and others we begin by observing others and seeing that they wish for happiness in the same way as we seek happiness. Also all sentient beings don't like to be unhappy and don't like suffering. We out of our habituation of being involved with ourselves, find it quite difficult to see this equality of self and others. So we should start out by putting a lot of effort into equalizing ourselves with others because it is not easy for a beginner to see the equality. Since we wish to eliminate suffering for ourselves and since there is no difference between ourselves and others, why not get rid of the suffering of other sentient beings? Since suffering is suffering, we should eliminate all suffering. If we like happiness and there is no difference between ourselves and others, we should delight in the happiness of all sentient beings and therefore work for the happiness of all.

We can have something wrong with our feet or with our hands, or have a headache, but whenever we have pain, we want to get rid of the pain. It's not like something is wrong with my hand or something is wrong with my foot; it is equally important to get rid of the suffering wherever it occurs. In the same way, since we are attached to them, then their suffering is unbearable.

The main point is that myself and all others are equal in that we want happiness and we want to get rid of suffering. Since we are equal, we should strive to obtain happiness for everyone and to eliminate the suffering of everyone.

Compassion

Then come some verses designed to clarify our doubts about equality of self and other. In verse 104 it says that since we are strive for gaining happiness and eliminating pain, then how should it be that we should train in compassion. When we train in compassion and become aware of the suffering of others, then we will also begin to feel sad and distressed at all the suffering of countless other sentient beings. If the point is for us to develop happiness and joy, then how can it be that training in compassion will lead to this?

It is true that compassion is by nature painful, but when compared to the suffering that comes about from wandering around in samsaric existence, this compassion leads to only a small amount of suffering. Since this suffering of compassion actually eliminates the great suffering of samsara, we should go through this pain. In the same way, a doctor might confer some temporary pain in the form of a short or operation to cure a serious illness. So we need to train in compassion although it is painful and we also need to make others aware that compassion is actually the method for eliminating all suffering.

How to Train in Exchanging Self and Others

106. *In this way his own sorrow was not destroyed by Supuspacandra[19] at the sacrifice of the sorrows of many, although he knew the way of the King.*

107. *Consequently [the Bodhisattvas, the compassionate], having transformed their mentalities (satarena), delighting in the tranquilizing of another's sorrow, plunge into the Avici hell like wild geese into a cluster of lotus.*

108. *When beings are delivered it is for them an ocean of joy which overwhelms all: What good is the insipid deliverance [of an Arhat or a Pratyekabuddha]?*

109. After having done something for the benefit of others, let there be neither excitement nor pride nor desire for subsequent merit: Let there be only thirst for the other's benefit.

110. Consequently, just as I protect myself from any evil which is occasioned by censure, so I create in others the thought of protection and the thought of compassion.

111. Because of habit, the concept of an 'I' becomes located in drops of semen, in blood, and in things belonging to another, although in reality the concept is false.

112. So why should the body of another not be taken as my own? It is not difficult, because of the remoteness of my own body.

113. After realizing that one is full of faults and that others are oceans of virtue, one should practice the rejection of the body and the acceptance of others.

114. The hand [with other parts] is loved as a member of the body: Why are living beings not loved as members of the universe?

115. Since the thought of "self" habitually is located in one's own body, although this has no selfhood, then why is selfhood not habitually conceived to be in others?

116. Having done something for the benefit of others, no excitement or pride or hope of merit is to be born, because one has only gratified one's self.

117. Consequently, as you wish to protect yourselves from pain, suffering, and so forth, let the thought of protection and the thought of compassion be practiced in the world.

118. Thus the Lord Avalokitishvara has given his own name to protect a man from even the fear of being timid in the Assembly.

119. One should not turn from difficulties because of regard for his reputation. One is without rest, protecting that reputation.

120. Whoever wishes to quickly rescue himself and another, should practice the supreme mystery: the exchanging of himself and the other.

121. Because of an excessive attachment to "self," even the slightest fear causes fear. Who would not hate that "self," who, like an enemy, is a carrier of fear;

122. who, desiring a defense against sickness, hunger, thirst, and the like, destroys birds, fish, animals, and stands as their antagonist;

123. who, for the sake of profit and honor would kill even his parents; who would steal even the Three Jewels, the inheritance which he has received; and who would be fuel for Avici:

124. What wise man would desire that "self"? Who would protect it? Who would worship it? Who would not regard it as an enemy? Who would honor it?

125. One thinks, "What shall I eat if I make an offering?" For the sake of the "self" he becomes a demon. One thinks, "What shall I give if I eat?" For the sake of another he becomes the King of the Gods.

126. Having injured another for the sake of the "self," one is cooked in hell:

Having injured himself for the sake of another, he is endowed with all prosperity.

127. *That wish for self-elevation which [creates] an evil destiny, baseness, and stupidity, [creates] a good destiny, honor, and intelligence when one has transferred it elsewhere.*

The text give the story of a bodhisattva Supuspacandra illustrating how we should train. This story comes from the *King of Samadhi* sutra where it explains that in a previous life the Buddha through his superior clairvoyance saw that if he was to go to the palace of the King and teach him the dharma, it would benefit a limitless number of sentient beings. However, he also saw in his vision that if he went there to teach, sooner or later the king would punish him and kill him. Nevertheless the Buddha chose to go to the palace and to teach the skillful means to the people there benefiting an incalculable mount of sentient beings and the king did eventually execute him.

When we become accustomed to comparing the pain of compassion with the pain of countless eons in samsara, the impulse of wanting to eliminate the suffering of others will be just as strong as the impulse to eliminate the suffering for oneself. Also the joy that we take in eliminating the suffering of others will be very great just as the joy of when one's own pain has been eliminated. So out of this great joy and strong impulse, we can enter even the deepest hell, just as a swan can land in a lotus pool (which traditionally is very dirty and polluted).

Since the realm of sentient beings is inexhaustible, then there would also be an inexhaustible joy. Because if one can benefit one sentient being, that will lead to great appreciation and delight. Then to benefit another one, there is again delight and joy. In this way it is an endless ocean of joy. Compared to this great happiness, reaching liberation just for oneself is small in comparison to the joy, happiness, and great bliss which is experienced by the bodhisattva who acts limitlessly for the benefit of all sentient beings.

One may wonder if there will be any kind of unfortunate circumstances connected to bodhisattva training. Will one feel conceited about being a bodhisattva? No, because one has the realization of oneself being the same as everyone else, having the insight of equality of oneself and other. Also one does not have hope for some wonderful effects of whatever one is doing in the future. One just thinks this is my job, this is what I am doing, and there is no difference between myself and others. Whenever one does as a bodhisattva is just eliminating suffering and that is the case for all sentient beings so there is no basis for conceit or hope for a goal in the future.

In the same way, as we like to avoid even the slightest discomfort we should eliminate even the most insignificant discomfort that can be suffered by others. We like to hear only pleasant things and the same way we should keep others from anything that is upsetting, and cause discomfort, just as we do for ourselves.

After having trained in the equality of I and other, we progress exchanging self and other, thinking oneself is the other and the other is oneself. Is this actually possible? Yes it is, because the idea of "me" is totally based on habituation which is described in verse 111. There is no way to find anything that we can call "I" in the sperm or the egg of the female. Due to the habituation of the mind, the mind's habits, we suddenly begin to conceive of these two objects as "me," although they actually belong to someone else. Because it is possible through mental habituation to conceive of "me" where there is no actual "me," in the future it will be possible to think of others as oneself.[20]

What are the benefits of exchanging oneself and others? First of all, if one holds onto the idea of "I" then there are many faults in thinking in this way. This belief in "I" will give rise to a lot of disturbing emotions which will cause suffering for both oneself and other. On the other hand, if we begin to consider others to be ourselves, a multitude of good qualities will ripen. We will be able to progress along the path of enlightenment and attain enlightenment. After attaining enlightenment, we will be able to help vast numbers of beings. This is possible because we are now in a situation where we are attached to the idea of "I" and there is no basis for "I." so we should entertain the idea that "I am other" an idea which has a great purpose and much benefit. One of the benefits is that if we are eating our own meal, we are not afraid that this going to be enjoyed by someone else in the future. In the same way, if we consider ourselves to be other, then when we engage in benefiting them, there is no chance that somebody else will reap the benefit of other since we are already doing the benefit of the other. It is like no one else is going to enjoy this meal. It's like we're eating our own meal, not being treated by someone else in a restaurant.

Directly killing an animal even to freed one self leads to negative karma. At this stage they now act solely for the benefit of others. So we can see the difference just by looking at these two.

128. Having ordered another for self-benefit, one experiences slavery: Having ordered himself for the benefit of another, he experiences power, and the like.

129. All of those who are in a condition of unhappiness in the world are that way because of desiring their own release. All of those who are in a condition of happiness in the world are that way from seeking the release of another.[21]

130. But why so much speaking? Let that difference be seen which is between the fool who is concerned with his own benefit, and the sage who creates benefit for another.

131. There is certainly no accomplishment, no Buddhahood, or even happiness in the realms of rebirth, for the one who does not exchange his own happiness for the sorrow of another.

Verse 128 lays out the path of a bodhisattva by saying that anyone who is interested in becoming free from suffering and attaining happiness by freeing everyone else from suffering, should train in exchanging self for others. This is a secret of oral instruction (of the practice of *exchanging oneself for others*) and what makes it possible to become free of suffering and give everyone happiness. If we train in this, this is what happens, if we don't, it won't. So we should train in this meditation.

To understand the importance of going through the process of eliminating suffering, we have to understand the problem of believing the body is "us." If we believe our body is ourselves, then even the most insignificant events will become a threat. We are afraid of just a single needle sticking our body and we try to stay away from that needle. Even the tinniest mosquito can become a great nuisance and we will try to run away from it. So we can see that there is quite a lot of misery connected to thinking, "My body is myself."

Out of cherishing our body we may become a hunter and kill many animals to feed this body thus causing great negative karma.[22] Treating our own body as important leads to many different situations leading to negative karma. This can lead to even wanting to kill one's own parents with the reasoning, "I need to take care of my body. For this reason we train in seeing our own body is an enemy, since it is the cause of a lot of fear and misfortune.

There are many reasons to begin in the training of exchanging oneself with others. To think "If I give myself away in this practice, what will I have left for myself to enjoy." is the thinking of hungry ghosts and demons and this attitude just leads to suffering for oneself and other. On the other hand, if we think, "If I myself take of this, then what will I have to give to others?" If we think in this way, then that is a fine quality, a characteristic of a true practitioner.

In the following verses it gives reasons for exchanging self for others. Simply sentient beings are obsessed with making themselves happy and because of that they create a great deal of misfortune for themselves. On the other hand, the buddhas who have reached full liberation from samsara are able to protect and help sentient beings by training for the benefit of others.

We need to train in exchanging self and others because without this it is impossible to reach enlightenment. Also if we want to accomplish the small things in this life, then we also need to train in exchanging ourselves for others. If we are a servant, then we should think that the person who has hired us is important and we should try to please them to get good pay. If we are the boss and have workers working for us still we need to exchange self and others to some extent thinking, "I should take good care of them and give them some presents, because if I don't they won't work hard. There is a great benefit from exchanging self and other in ordinary daily situations.

Gaining True Freedom

132. *Not even considering the next world, our welfare here does not prosper. The workman does not do that for which he is paid; the master does not give wages to the workman.*

133. *After forsaking the origin of mutual happiness (the flowering of happiness whether seen or unseen), the infatuated grasp at terrible sorrow, because sorrow is mutual.*

134. *Whatever calamities there are, and whatever sorrows and fears come to the world, they are all the result of attachment to "self." Why is that attachment mine?*

135. *Not having extinguished "self," one is not able to extinguish sorrow; just as one who has not extinguished a fire is not able to extinguish the burning.*

136. *It follows that for the sake of tranquilizing my own sorrow, and for the tranquilizing of the other's sorrow, I give myself to others and I accept others like myself.*

137. *That I am another is a certainty well understood: Accept it, O mind! Having cast off all for the sake of beings, nothing else is to be considered by you tomorrow.*

138. *It is not suitable to employ sight [and similar faculties] for self-benefit, because the eyes, and so forth, are theirs. It is not suitable to move the hands for self-benefit, because they belong to others.*

139. *After giving yourselves to other beings, whatever you see in the body which may be applied to the advantage of others, is to be taken away from it.*

If all the pain, fear, and misery that can come to us in this world is the result of wishing well for ourselves. Examining this we conclude this state of affairs and so shouldn't we begin to consider grasping at self as the true demon that we just need to expel.

After expelling this demon we should begin to think, "I am the servant, I am under the control of everyone else." We should take care not to have any selfish ideas and beliefs, since they are the cause of suffering. Whenever we find anything that can be of benefit to sentient beings, we should just take it from ourselves and give it away to sentient beings. This is generally how to train in exchanging oneself and others.

There are two kinds of awakening mind: ultimate bodhichitta and relative bodhichitta. Ultimate bodhichitta will be described in the next chapter on wisdom. In this chapter on meditation we explain how to practice and train in relative bodhichitta. We have discussed how to give up worldly life, how to abandon selfish thinking, and how to cultivate the good qualities of a solitary retreat. These are the circumstances for reaching the main part of practicing relative bodhichitta. The two methods for actually training in relative bodhichitta considering oneself and other as equal and training in exchanging oneself for others.

All sentient beings, no matter who or what they are, possess the basic element of enlightenment (Buddha-nature) and so they are therefore potentially endowed with perfect wisdom and wakefulness. So no matter how low and inferior a sentient being may be, still this being has the seed for enlightenment. Although sentient beings possess this basic element of enlightenment, these are not present due to disturbing emotions and obscurations. Whenever disturbing emotions are present it become impossible to see clearly what is good and what is bad. Whenever there are disturbing emotions, the mind does not function in a way that is truly wholesome. Being under the power of disturbing emotions is by nature ignorance and stupidity. This kind of ignorance shows itself in conceiving one's self as "I am."

From now on we will mainly discuss how to deal with the stupidity which is concerned with how there are a lot of disadvantages of conceiving of a self and holding onto ego. When we hold onto ego, it will seem more important to be happy ourselves and it won't matter much whether other sentient beings are happy. To counteract this unwholesome mental attitude, we should train in considering ourselves and others equal and train in exchanging ourselves for others.

When there is ego clinging, there is a multitude of faults and defects that we will experience for ourselves. For instance, when we hold onto ego, there will be the natural tendency to consider those who are in an inferior position as not so valuable as oneself. We will feel superior to those not in a fortunate position. The ignorance that accompanies the clinging to self, prevents one to actually see how one feels superior and how one looks down on others. Clinging to ego causes us to have a , competitive attitude towards others by thinking, "I can do better than this person." The ignorance of ego clinging prevents us from seeing that we are actually competing with those who are in an equal situation to us. Also ego clinging will cause us to feel jealous of those in a superior position and feel it is not justified how they are in a superior position. When we are trained in exchanging self for others by putting ourselves in the position o someone else, we can begin to think, "I will trade with this person, I am now this superior person. and then we can examine how much benefit there is of being jealous at myself." In the same way, when exchanging self with a person who is in an equal position can show us the impulses and patterns of behavior that expresses itself as competitiveness.

Exchanging Self with an Inferior

140. After establishing "selfhood" in the most lowly, and the stranger in the "self," both envy and pride may arise without scruple of the mind.

141. He is honored: I am not. I am not rich like him. He is praised: I am blamed. I am sorrowful: He is the happy one.

142. I am engaged in labors, while he remains at ease. He is indeed great in the world: I am indeed base and without virtues.

143. What can be done by one without virtues? Yet everyone may not be endowed with virtues. There are those to whom I am base: There are those to whom I am superior.

144. If my conduct or my teaching has fallen into ruin, it is because of the power of disturbing emotions, not because of my own will. I am to be cured, if it is possible; I have surely accepted the pain.

145. If I cannot he cured by this ["self"], why does he despise me? What to me are these virtues? Because of such virtues he is endowed with "self."

146. Has he only compassion for those men who dwell in the mouths of the beasts of prey in an evil place? In pride of virtue he strives to surpass the distant sages.

147. Having seen one equal to himself, he must strive for the increase of his own superiority. By quarreling he is to obtain profit ,and honor for himself.

148. May my virtues become manifest everywhere in the world: But whatever virtues he may have, let them not be heard anywhere.

149. Let my faults be hidden that there may be honor to me, but let there be none for him. Benefits have now been obtained by me: I am honored, but he is not.

150. So behold you fully although it is late the one who is ill-treated, laughed at

by every man, reviled: Thus was he bent down.
151. Indeed, what a comparison between that wretched one and myself! What kind of learning has he? What wisdom? beauty? family? wealth?

Also, if we exchange with someone in an inferior position,[23] we can become aware of how harmful looking down on someone is. More specifically to meditate exchanging self with someone in an inferior position, we should very honestly and straightforwardly put ourselves in the position of this person. Then try to look with jealousy at ourselves (the superior one). Seeing exactly how we feel annoyed with how we looked down upon us we really become aware of the faults that we have in our ordinary way of behaving and thinking. Also when we exchange with someone in an equal position, we see how we are always trying to compete with someone else. Our behavior becomes more clear when we exchange with someone else. Then we should exchange with someone in a higher position and try to look down and see all the defect that we have and how it creates pride and a feeling of superiority. We can then clearly see all kinds of inferior qualities that we ourselves possess. Through this kind of training of exchanging self and other we become able to actually notice our thoughts, and thereby we can abandon them. When we abandon these thoughts, we develop a truly kind heart And are able to give up stupidity and ignorance. Although these feelings of superiority, competitiveness, and jealousy are disturbing emotions, we do exchange training to notice and contemplate these thoughts so we are actually cultivating the disturbing emotions at this point.

Exchanging Self with a Superior Person

152. Having heard in this way about my virtue, my honors having been recited everywhere, my hair has become stiff with the thrill of pleasure: I enjoy the uttermost happiness.
153. If there is any advantage which he may have, it is to be forcibly seized by us. We will give him only maintenance if he will serve us.
154. He is to be shaken from his happiness. He is forever to be yoked to our anguish. A hundred times, because of him, we all [have endured] that state of anguish which is samsara.
155. You have passed through immeasurable eons searching for your own well-being, and you have gained only sorrow as the result of this gigantic effort.
156. Turn, then, according to my entreaty, without hesitation! You shall see the results at a later time, because the word of the Buddha is true.
157. If you previously had made this to be your objects striving for the fulfillment of a Buddha liberation would have occurred, and this condition

of life would not have occurred.

158. Therefore, as you located the Ego in drops of sperm and of blood, in things belonging to another, so now let it be found in others.

159. After you have become another's spy, use whatever thing you see in the body that is advantageous to another, only for the sake of stealing it for him.

160. Be jealous of your own self, realizing that it is happy while another is unhappy, that it is exalted while another is base, that another works while it does not.

161. Remove the "self" from happiness. Concentrate upon the unhappiness of others. Notice when he is deceitful, and what he does.

162 Let the sin committed by him fall upon his own head; and let him confess even the slightest sin to the Great Buddha.

163. Make dark his reputation by speaking of the superior reputation of others; and make him labor like a base slave in the service of others.

164. He is not to be praised because of a particle of adventitious virtue; he is full of faults: Treat him in such a way that his virtue will not be known by anyone.

We try to put ourselves in a lower position and look with jealousy at ourselves. When we do this, we become able to see how we actually look down on others. When we imagine that now we are this person that is lower we can actually clearly see how we despise and lack compassion for inferior persons and it becomes obvious what great faults are created out of this unkind and disparaging attitude.

Then exchanging with an equal person allows us to examine competition. Because of our ego clinging, when there is someone of an equal position whether it be in material wealth, in intelligence, or personal qualities, we will have a natural inclination to try to come out better than this other person. So when we now put ourselves in the position of someone else, we can see all these faults and be aware of them and thereby be able to actually abandon them.

Next we try to put ourselves in a position to one who is superior making it obvious of the faults and defects of being proud. It become obvious in this exchange that we will feel jealousy and try to compete with others.

To counteract the disturbing emotions, we use the opposite to these disturbing emotions as the antidote. This is what is being explained in great detail in the text. When we are clinging to ego, there will always be a low of disturbing emotions because clinging to ego is by nature ignorance. Although we have all these disturbing emotions due to the stupidity of ego clinging, we do not recognize these defects. So to actually recognize these faults and be able to abandon them, we train using pride as the antidote for jealously. We also train in abandoning competitiveness with exchanging self for others thus reducing the disturbing emotions.

Summary of the Practice

165. *Summing it up, whatever injury you did to others for the sake of* "self," *let that evil fall upon the* "self" *for the sake of beings.*

166. *He is not to be given the power by which he may be at ease. Treat him as a young bride to be restrained; one that is purchased, frightened, guarded.*

167. *"Do thus. Stand so! This is not to be done by you!" In this way he is to be subdued, he is to be punished when in transgression.*

168. *"Since you will not do to this mind as you are told, then I shall punish you. Because of you all faults have found refuge.*

169. *"Where will you go? All of your pride is beheld by me, and I destroy you. That earlier time is past when I was not satiated by you.*

170. *"Now abandon hope that you still have self-interest of your own: without considering your inconvenience, I have sold you to others.*

171. *"Indeed, if heedlessly I do not give you to beings, you, without hesitation, will deliver me to the guards of hell,*

172. *"and many times have I been delivered thus by you, and I have been long afflicted. Remembering your hostile actions, I destroy you, slave of self-interest!"*

173. *The* "self" *is not to be loved if the* "self" *is loved by you. If the* "self" *is to be protected it ought not to be concerned with its protection.*

174. *The more that is done for the protection of the body, the more it falls and the more severe its suffering;*

175. *But even when it has fallen, this entire earth is not able to satisfy its longings. Who can fulfill its desire?*

176. *Because of desire for the impossible there is born disturbing emotions and the frustration of hope; but whoever is without hope has everywhere an ageless good fortune.*

177. *Consequently, no opportunity is to be given for the growth of the body's desire. Auspicious, indeed, is that thing which is not seized because of its desirability.*

178. *That inert thing, whose end is reduction to ashes, is moved by another. Why then is that filthy, horrible image seized by me?*

179. *What is that contrivance to me, whether it is living or it is dead? What is the difference between it and a clod of earth? Why do you not perish, O Ego!*

180. *Because of partiality for the body, sorrow is experienced in vain. What is either the hatred or the affection of that thing which is equal to a stick of wood?*

181. It has no attachment and no hatred, whether it is thus guarded by me or whether it is eaten by feeding vultures. How, then, can I be attached to it?

182. Whose is the anger when it is abused? And whose is the delight when it is honored? Of what use, if in reality it knows nothing, is any effort that I make?

183. Those who love this body are those who are indeed my friends! Yet all love their own bodies, so why do I not love them?

What is it that we actually need to achieve by training in exchanging self for others? In these verses we are actually instructing ourselves. This needs to be done in a very relaxed and kind-hearted manner. We need to instruct ourselves and give ourselves some good advice. We begin with thinking how we have been chasing around in samsara always wishing, "I must get rich." or "I should be really intelligent" or "I should get in a perfect situation." We've gone through all kinds of hardship to reach our goal, but we've never gotten anything out of it. On the contrary, in our pursuit we have only increased our suffering with old age, sickness, and death.

What we need to do now is give up the old way of thinking and engage in a new way. Seeing the defects of our old way of thinking, it becomes easy to engage in the new way, namely, striving for the benefit of others. The good effects of this new way is certain since the word of the Buddha is infallible.

In the past we have always considered ourselves to be more important than others. But now the attention has shifted so we are now only interested in achieving good for others. Whatever we have, we can now steal from ourselves and give to others. Whatever defects of ours that become obvious, we use to consider ourselves inferior and everyone else as superior. This is how to train in shifting the emphasis from self to others.

We need to check ourselves continuously, taking care to notice what we are thinking, what we are saying, and what we are doing physically. This kind of mindfulness should be ongoing. Sometimes others will do something wrong to us and when that happens, we should not see it as a wrong done to us, but as something that happens because of the unfortunate patterning that we have brought upon ourselves. On the other hand, when we do the tiniest wrong, we should not hesitate to proclaim it widely to others.

We should begin by advising ourselves what to do in a very soft and gentle way. Explaining the faults that come about when we consider ourselves important and desiring only our own happiness. We have been through this reasoning seeing clearly how it is that it is a mistake to being happiness only to ourselves because it will harm others.

If we cannot give up this thinking pattern the next step is to use a stronger means as suggested in verse 168.

This wishing good for ourselves has always produced a lot of misfortune. This wanting happiness for ourselves is what put us through all the pain in the hell realms. Now we have seen this fact, it is not anyone like it was in the past where we didn't realize the consequences of cherishing ourselves. Now we see that cherishing ourselves is just cheating us and leading us to hell. If we forget through lack of mindfulness; then again we shall be taken to the hell realms.

If we wish to take care of ourselves, one wants to avoid any danger to oneself, then one should help others. If one helps others, then oneself will also be safe. In the same way, if one wants to be happy, one will make others happy. in this way, we must change our attitude.

There is a lot of misfortune connected to being attached to our mind. Also there is a lot of suffering that comes about when we are attached to our body. If we consider the mind to be very important, then there will be a lot of disturbing emotion based on this attachment which will lead to unwholesome behavior. If we wish to do good to the body, we will not refrain from doing what is unwholesome and thereby accumulate a lot of evil. In these verses it shows how there is not reason to put that emphasis on being attached to the body. No matter how much we try to do good to the body, it will end up having not effect. Actually the body will get in a worse and worse condition, no matter how hard we try to please it. The craving for bodily happiness will increase the feeling of pain. If we just go on like this without any kind of restraint, then we will not accomplish what we wish for. Nothing of this earth will give us the happiness and comfort that we strive for. Instead we develop some kind of appreciation, that we have already enough.

So we need the skillful means to develop feelings of ease and feeling of being satisfied with our situation and what we have. If we apply a lot of effort to the pursuit of satisfying the body, then no matter what we do, our body will end up as ashes and dust. All the efforts and hardships that we go through will have no result, and the unwholesome behavior that we get used to in this way will end up harming us. So there is no reason to put effort into pleasing the body.

The Resolve to Raise Bodhichitta

184. With indifference, then, I renounce the body for the welfare of the world. Henceforth it is borne, although it is of many faults, like an instrument of Karma.

185. Enough of worldly activities because of it! Turning aside from apathy and from indolence, and having remembered the Discourse on Heedfulness (apramada), I follow the learned ones.

186. To destroy hindrance, therefore, I engage in contemplation, a perpetual asylum for the mind which has withdrawn from the false path.

In verse 184 there is the instruction. At this point we must let go of the body and without attachment give it away to sentient beings thinking that now this body is a possession of others to carry out what pleases them and makes them happy. I am now giving my body away for the benefit of others.

Our body does have a lot of flaws and defects. Based on cherishing our body, we create a lot of evil and experience suffering and with this body we wander in samsara. Even though it has a lot of faults and we give it away, still take care of it considering it just as a tool for accomplishing the benefit of others. It is just like having a hammer, a saw or other ordinary tools which are useful when we want to build something. But we don't think of our tools as great treasures. In the same way, although our body has defects, we should when giving it away to others, take care of it and employ it just as one uses a tool to build something.

In summary, there are great faults in being attached to our mind and a great fault in being attached to our body. The text shows us how to give up this attachment to mind and body by exchanging self for others. We need to think, Now I have entered the activities of a bodhisattva and when I do this I have to rely on conscientiousness. Being conscientious, I will need to greatly work at diligence also. Being diligent I will have to turn away from sleep and mental dullness.

So I just like the compassionate sons of the Buddha and the great bodhisattvas, I shall accept whatever I encounter. This is what to train in, in order to eliminate suffering. This constant effort night and day will bring an end to suffering. To bring an end to obscuration and stupidity, I need to continually see that I have not falling into the mistaken way. I need to take care that I have entered the right path that I don't slip from it, or proceed along a false path. To do this I will need to be aware and diligent.

Questions

Question: How do we know when we are sufficiently developed in our Shamatha meditation to go on to Vipashyana meditation?

Rinpoche: It is not good if we stay with Shamatha meditation and never begin Vipashyana meditation. Because Vipashyana is actually being able to uproot the disturbing emotions, Vipashyana is what establishes us in liberation. For this reason we need to begin Vipashyana, but this Vipashyana meditation needs to be grounded in the calm abiding of Shamatha meditation. What are the signs of having reached a stable mind in Shamatha meditation? The signs are that you can rest your mind whenever you want it to rest, that your have little trouble in letting go and being at ease at will, that you do not often experience the faults of dullness and agitation in your meditation. When you do not have dullness or agitation often and that your mind is easy and open, then that is a sign that your mind has some kind of stability and that is a sign that your are ready for Vipashyana meditation.

Question: How does forsaking attachment to friends and relatives relate to the relationship one has for one's children?

Rinpoche: There is the feeling of attachment and there is the feeling of wanting to benefit others. We need to understand that wishing good for our children is not something undesirable, but is something good. It is all right to think, "I wish that my children will be healthy, they will have a good education, and that they will have a good life." That is simply wishing them well and is giving up nothing. On the other hand thinking, "I must always be with my children and I cannot live without them." is attachment and this is not healthy. If one wishes well for one's children, then its fine and there's nothing to give up.

Question: Can you say something about enlightenment.

Rinpoche: There are various religious traditions in the world. Non-Buddhist traditions often believe that enlightenment is God, a supernatural power which if one prays to this God, then that God will be pleased and will grant one whatever one wishes. They also believe that if one does not pray to that God and does not keep contact with that God, the God will not be pleased and one will not get what one wishes. So this is the theist view of enlightenment. But in Buddhism, enlightenment is noting outside, it is nothing other than our own mind. Sometimes our mind is polluted, sometimes the good qualities of our mind do not manifest, but when our mind is purified, then all these special qualities of enlightenment will unfold. The word for enlightenment in Tibetan is "sang gay" with each syllable having a meaning. The first syllable sang means "to purify" and the second syllable gay means "fully" so reaching enlightenment is when all the temporary thoughts of the mind have been dispelled by the power of meditation and all the excellent qualities of the mind have unfolded fully.

Question: Can you say something about busyness?

Rinpoche: If we look at our life, we see that we are actually always in pursuit of something, always busy doing something. When night comes, we go to bed thinking we didn't really finish that job and we'll have to get up really early tomorrow to do it. Then the next day we work worrying about whether we will finish our job. We go on this way without ever really completing the project especially in modern life. Then we feel unhappy when we have no project or job. So we're suffering and if we are busy and unhappy when we are not busy. This is what is understood by the suffering of busyness. This is due because our mind is never satisfied thinking, "I will be happy if I have $ 1,000." Then when we get it we think, "No, I need $ 2,000." We are always thinking that it is quite enough, we need more. This is the impulse that causes suffering in human beings.

Chapter 9

The Perfection of Wisdom

A Guide to the Bodhisattva's Way of Life gives three methods for working with bodhichitta. First, it discusses how to develop bodhichitta that is unborn. Second, it teaches how to develop bodhichitta once it has been born. Finally, it gives the method of how to develop bodhichitta over and over again to prevent it from decreasing. The first and the second methods have already been discussed. In this chapter we will discuss how develop bodhichitta over and over again. In order to do so we are given the practices of enthusiastic effort, meditative concentration, and prajna or wisdom. Of these three, the most important one is prajna.

There are two words for wisdom, *prajna* and *jnana*. Jnana is the wisdom of absolute realization. Prajna, on the other hand, refers to wisdom which is gained through analytical reasoning. Generally, prajna is the ability to grasp something which is very difficult to understand. That is the normal definition of prajna. But in this particular case, prajna is related to the superior understanding of all phenomena which is beyond the capacity of ordinary beings like ourselves.

So this chapter begins with:

1. The Buddha taught that this multitude [of Virtues] is all for the sake of wisdom (prajna); hence, by means of one's desire for the extinction of sorrow, let wisdom arise.

The purpose of all perfection (paramita) practice is to cultivate prajna. The practice of generosity, moral conduct, patience, enthusiastic effort, and meditative concentration are all aimed towards developing our prajna. Why do we have to develop prajna? It is because samsaric conditions have deluded us so that we have not grasped ultimate realization. The development of prajna is the only way to remove this ignorance or confusion. Therefore, the goal of all paramita practice is to realize, experience, and develop this prajna within ourselves.

Because we are conditioned by samsara, we are confused and we experience suffering. We can stop our pain by developing our wisdom which is free from any ignorance, confusion, or delusion. Unless we realize that the nature of all phenomena is illusion, we will not be able to free ourselves from suffering. So to have this kind of understanding, it is necessary to cultivate prajna.

Relative and Ultimate Truth

The method used in the text for developing prajna is the teaching on the two truths: the deceptive or relative truth (Tib. *kunzop*) and ultimate truth (Tib. *dondam*). Relative truth refers to whatever is apparent. Everything that we perceive at this moment is known as the relative truth. The ultimate truth refers to the essential nature of our perceptions. Neither the relative truth nor the ultimate truth are unreal; they are both real. The relative truth is true on the relative level, and the ultimate truth is real on the absolute or ultimate level.

Both relative and ultimate truth are valid on different levels. This can be explained with the example of a man who falls asleep in his bed and dreams of an elephant. Now, when he awakens and shares his dream with his friends, was there really an elephant in his room? No, there wasn't a real elephant in the room. Rationally, we could see that the room was too small to accommodate an elephant. Furthermore, if there were an elephant it would have broken the bed. So through reasoning we can prove that there was no elephant present. If we looked for an elephant in the brain of the dreamer, we can see that it could not possibly hold an elephant. So, through reasoning to examining the outer, inner, and in-between realities of the dreamer, we find that no real elephant could exist. So that explanation proves the non-existence of the elephant. We can see there was no elephant. If there were no elephant, then there was no cessation of the elephant either. In other words, what was not there could not be asked to leave?

However, we cannot deny that the man dreamt of an elephant. In the dream he experienced the elephant. So according to the dream, we accept there was an elephant. In other words on the relative level, we accept the existence of the elephant while on an ultimate level there wasn't an elephant. Inside and outside the body of the man we know there wasn't an elephant. Since there was no elephant to begin with, there is also no cessation of an elephant. That is on the ultimate level. Whatever we perceive is real according to the perceiver. It seems very true. That is the relative level. But the object of our perception, the perception itself, is not concrete and has no solid reality. This is the ultimate level. So this is the explanation of the relative and ultimate truth.

The Emptiness of Self

Those who have practiced meditation may understand the meaning of emptiness (Skt. *shunyata*). Those new to the dharma are sometimes confused by the idea of emptiness. When someone explains that everything is emptiness, one might ask, "How can that be possible? We are able to see things, we're able to touch things and so on." Because the topic of emptiness can be such a difficult subject to explain, it is easier if we use analytical methods. So here is a brief explanation of emptiness using rational analysis and logic.

If you look at my hand you will see that this hand is real. No matter how many people are in this room, they will all agree that this hand exists. It feels very real, it moves, it can do work. For example, it is able to lift the book, and turn the pages. But using pure reasoning, this isn't a solid hand. For example, this is my thumb, it isn't a hand, it is a thumb. These fingers are not a hand, they are an index finger, a middle finger, a ring finger, a little finger. What about the outer part of this thing we call a hand? There is skin and inside the skin is flesh and inside that there is bone. So what really is it that you call a hand? So, logically speaking there is no such thing as a solid, firm existence of this hand that you earlier believed was real. Also there is no extra object that is known as the hand other than the combination of thumb, index finger, middle finger, ring, flesh, bone and skin that we have labeled "a hand." No extra thing exists as hand. So the idea of "hand" is emptiness or nonexistence.

If you go further, and ask "does that only relate to the hand?" No, you can use that logical reasoning on anything. For example, you could say, "now I can accept that the hand does not exist. But my the thumb exists" But the thumb does not exist because if you use logic the thumb consists of the nail, the joint, the skin, flesh, and so on. So there is no true existence of thumb as well. You can use this same logical reasoning with anything that seems to exist and prove the nonexistence of that thing. You could apply it to the left hand, the right hand, the body or the head. Eventually everything that seems to be real or existent is discovered to be simply an idea or name labeled by the mind. So there is no true existence. Everything, in fact, is emptiness but to our perception it appears that everything exists. Just like the example of the dreamer. Within the dream the person was able to perceive the elephant, but it did not really exist.

Next, the text explains the relative and the absolute truth in verse 2:

2. *It is understood that truth is of two kinds: relative truth and absolute truth. True reality is beyond the range of understanding (buddhi); so understanding is called relative.*

So the ultimate truth cannot be realized at the relative level. It is realized through applying profound meditative practice called *samadhi.* Currently we can only understand relative truth and the ultimate level can not be understood by reasoning only.

Verses 3 and 4 explain that the yogi actually tries to realize the two truths, the ultimate truth, by applying meditative practice.

3. *Consequently, the world is seen to be divided into two parts, that of the yogi and that of the mundane; and perforce the mundane world is distinguished from the world of the yogi.*
4. *Even yogis are distinguished by differences of mental power; but because the purpose of all of them is the same, the aim of all of them is valid.*

So there are two kinds of individuals: ordinary beings who are unfamiliar with meditation and for them everything they perceive seems to be real. Then there is the yogi or the practitioner who does not perceive phenomena like ordinary beings. The yogi knows that everything that yogi perceives is not real. The yogi is able to explain the nonexistence of the phenomena perceived by ordinary beings. But enlightened beings have presented teachings for the yogis. Step by step, the level of the ultimate truth is presented from the Hinayana to the Mahayana. The Mahayana view is presented in the Mind-only (Skt. *Chittamatra*) tradition and the Middle-way (Skt. *Madhyamaka*) tradition. In each step a more complicated explanation is developed further by the enlightened beings for the yogis to follow.

So in the very beginning at the Hinayana, the idea of emptiness is presented in a simplistic way with only a partial presentation of emptiness given. That idea is presented just as with the example of the hand. Then step by step analytical methods are used to explain the nonexistence of the hand, of the finger, right down to the level of the atom. In the Hinayana tradition, we are told that the atom exists and therefore the accumulation of atoms is known as a *skandha* or heap.

At a higher level of the Hinayana tradition, the emptiness of phenomena is proved through understanding that aggregates are accumulations of many small particles or atoms. These combine together which make up the aggregate, and therefore we come to the point of the egolessness of self.

But the Chittamatra tradition goes deeper so even the particle known as an atom has no specific size or measurement. One cannot really give a fixed size to the atom and with this reasoning one can prove that the atom itself is mind made and that outer existence of everything is simply a mental projection. So the Chittamatra tradition comes to the point that no outer existence is possible, it is merely made by mind. But the Chittamatra adherents are attached to the existence of the mind; having said that everything in outer existence is made of small particles that are made by mind. So in the Chittamatra tradition there is attachment to the existence of mind.

Again, when we go to a deeper level of understanding and search for the mind, we cannot find the mind. Through reasoning we have the eye consciousness, nose consciousness, tongue consciousness, body consciousness and mind consciousness. In the Madhyamaka tradition, mind itself is nonexistent because when we search for it there is no such thing as a solid firm being we can find or identify as "mind."

So we have here the system of debate. We should not misunderstand debate. The system of debate has developed to help a practitioner to understand the different views which we have explained.

5. *Things are seen by the world and they are assumed to be real; it is not realized that they are only illusion (maya). Thus the quarrel between the yogi and the worldly.*

To give an example of this verse, while ordinary beings are able to perceive all that exists in the phenomenal world, they take it to be real. Yogis are also able to perceive outer phenomena just as ordinary beings do, but yogis understand that everything that they perceive is dreamlike, like an illusion. That is the difference between ordinary people's perceptions of the outer phenomena and the perception of the yogi.

6 *Even sense perception (pratyaksha) with its [classical] argument based upon the proof of form and so forth, is not in accord with the criteria of valid knowledge (pramana). This is false, like the argument that purity and so on, is impurity and so on*

7. *For the sake of his appearance in the world things were taught by the Lord to be momentarily real. It is not because of the relative truth if this is contradicted.*

8. *There is no corruption because of the relative truth of the Yogi, since they distinguish reality from the world. Otherwise, there would be worldly afflictions for them, as in the case of unclean women.*

9. *On the other hand, how is there any value regarding so-called reality, even*

concerning the Conqueror, who is equated to illusion? If a being is the same as illusion, how much less is it to be born? or to have died?

10. *As long as there is a totality of causes, to that very extent, illusion conceals; for how is a profound continuity of elements really real?*

11. *There is no evil [it is argued] in the destruction of a man who is illusion, because of the absence of thought; but because thought is affected by illusion, sin and merit have arisen.*

12. *The encounter of illusion and thought is not due to the power of spells (mantras) and so forth. Illusion is of different kinds, and the encounter has a variety of causes.*

13. *From what single cause is the power of everything derived? For one in transmigration, release comes both by means of absolute truth and by means of truth truth.*

14. *Even the Buddha [it is argued] is thus in transmigration; what good, then, is the course of Enlightenment! When causes are not cut off, certainly illusion itself is not cut off;*

15. *but because of the cutting off of causes, being exists no more as the result of relative truth. As soon as there is no moving to and fro [or error], by what means is illusion perceived?*

16. *When illusion does not exist for you, then how is it perceived? It is just a fabrication of thought if it is otherwise than true reality.*

17. *When even thought is illusion, then what is seen? and by whom? For it is taught by the Lord of the Earth that thought does not behold thought.*

These verses are a debate between the Shravaka tradition, which believes that the smallest particle exists and that outer phenomena also exist because everything is an accumulation of these smallest particles and the Madhyamaka tradition, which believes that even these smallest particles do not exist. The question debates in this section is if all phenomena are if all phenomena are unreal, then the offerings to the buddhas and bodhisattvas are unreal. Likewise if one murders a sentient being, that act should not lead to accumulated negative karma because it is all illusion. When we are making an offering, that offering in itself is illusion. Therefore the accumulation of merit from the offering is also an illusion. There is no merit that actually exists separate from the illusion itself. Similarly, if you destroy a life, you and the being you kill are an illusion. So you accumulate illusory negative karma related to this illusion on a relative level, but there is no extra negative karma that is separate from that illusion.

So there is this debate. The Madhyamaka tradition makes this argument through logical reasoning. Because it is presented with logical reasoning, those unfamiliar with practice may find that logical reasoning becomes a game. However, it is very important to understand the nature of nonexistence, particularly when we are going to practice meditation. When we rest our mind, to understand the nature of your mind through the practice of Mahamudra, or Dzogchen this understanding of nonexistence according to the Madhyamaka method of logical reasoning is very essential.

The Egolessness of Self

Our discussion of the ninth chapter prajna deals with relative truth and absolute truth. Absolute truth refers to the sense that everything is emptiness. In this section there a discussion about this state of emptiness as argued from different points of view. The different truths debated are from the Shravaka school, which is the Hinayana school, and the Madhyamaka school and Chittamatra or Mind-only school. In the last chapter we talked about the debate with the Hinayana school and today we will discuss the Chittamatra school.

The view of the Chittamatra school is that all the outer phenomena as well as the inner physical body are only the manifestations of mind. Anything that appears firm concrete or solid, regardless of whether it is outside or inside our body does not exist. External physical forms are only a projection of the mind. That it is the general belief of Chittamatra school.

The view that outer phenomena does not exist but is a mere projection of our mind is illustrated with the example of a dream. One may dream of a house, mountains and so forth. However, the physical existence of these dream objects does not exist, it is simply a manifestation of our mind.

This understanding of outer phenomena simply being a manifestation of our mind is very important and in itself has quality. For example all that teachings of the Mahamudra or Dzogchen practices depend upon practicing meditation on the nature of the mind. The understanding that everything is the manifestation of our mind helps tremendously in the practice of Mahamudra. This Mind-only tradition is also explained in many sutras, such as Lankara sutra from the Shakyamuni Buddha.

In this tradition, the view of the Chittamatra school is presented in a manner that states that mind itself is real. Therefore, from the point of view of the Madhyamaka school, the Chittamatra school has not come far enough to understand the nonexistence of the mind itself, because the mind itself is thought of as real.

It is important to note that within the Chittamatra tradition there are two schools, the *nyam drun pa* (*drun* means "unreal" or "deceptive") and the *nyam chen pa* (*chen* means "true" or "real"). Beginning with the Chittamatra school of the *namchenpa* which begins with verse 15:

17. *When even thought (chitta) is illusion (maya), then what is seen? and by whom? For it is taught by the Lord of the Earth that thought does not behold thought.*
18. *As the blade of the sword does not cut itself, neither does the mind know itself. If it is thought that the self is like a lamp which illuminates,*
19. *that lamp cannot be illuminated, since it is not covered by darkness. Indeed, that which is dark is not like a crystal either: Being dark, it does not expect anything else.*
20. *Thus when light is seen by others, it is seen irrespective of darkness. It may not make itself dark by itself when it is not dark.*
21. *Likewise, what darkness cad make itself dark by itself? It cannot make itself dark by itself when it is not dark.*
22. *The experience of knowing that a lamp illumines is affirmed by knowledge. The experience of knowing that intelligence illumines, by what is this affirmed?*
23. *That it is illumined or not illumined, as long as it is seen by no one whatsoever, is as uselessly affirmed as the charm of a barren woman's daughter.*
24. *If there is no act of self-knowledge, how is consciousness remembered? Memory is from an association with an exterior perception, as the poison is to the rat.*
25. *The self [it is argued] is illumined by observing its association with proximate causes; but the jar which is found by the use of magical ointment is not that ointment itself.*
26. *In this way, what is seen, what is heard, what is known, is, indeed, never denied; but still this hypothesis does not destroy the cause of sorrow.*

The Chittamatra school accepts the Madhyamaka view that all the outer phenomenon does not exist. However, the Chittamatra argument is that there must be a mind that is subjected to confusion. So the reply to this is in stanza 22:

No mind at all can behold (a truly existing consciousness).
Thus it is meaningless to discuss
such illuminating itself or not.
Like the looks of the daughter of a barren women.

If you try to look at what the mind is, you are unable to actually find or see the mind. Therefore the issue of whether it is good or bad, clear or dark, is like discussing the existence of the daughter of a barren woman. If a woman cannot give birth to a child at all, what is the point of speculating whether her daughter would be attractive or ugly when she cannot exist at all.

The next point is based on the view of Chittamatra of *nam drung pa* which starts at verse 26:

27. *If it is affirmed that the thing that is not illusion is none other than that which is created by thought—if that is the real, how is it other than a fabrication of illusion if it really does not exist?*

28. *If that which is seen is as unreal as illusion, then so is the one who sees the mind. If the realms of rebirth are based on reality, they must be as different [from reality] as the sky is different from reality*

29. *When reality is based on nonreality, how can you be the one who acts? Indeed, your thought needs one companion, the nonexistent.*

30. *As long as thought is destitute of an object, then all are Buddhas. Moreover, when there is only thought, what merit is obtainable?*

Generally there is not a vast difference in the two Chittamatra schools, the *nonchenpa* and *nandrunpa*. Using the example of dreaming of an elephant, the Chittamatras of the namchenpa school believe that the mind is the one that is experiencing the elephant in the dream. Now the Chittamatra school of nondrunpa says that there is the mind which is observing things happening so the dream experience is not the actual or real mind, it is *drun* meaning "unreal" or "deceptive."

So here the Madhyamaka school is conversing with the Chittamatra school of the namdrunpa. The Chittamatra school of the namdrunpas says that mind has to exist in order to observe or experience all the objects of mind or outer phenomena. The Madhyamaka school argues here that this mind that the Mind-only school believes exists does not exist.

The three schools of the Chittamatra, Vaibhashika, and the Sautrantika are known for believing in the existence of mind. The discussions here are between the Madhyamaka school and these three schools beginning with verse 30 to 34:

31. *But [it is argued] if it is understood that thought is only the likeness of illusion, how is passion turned aside? Even as she is created, the magician falls in love with the maya woman.*

32. *Indeed, the impression of passion, still to be understood by the magician, has not been worn out. In that moment of beholding her, his impression of the Void (Janya) is weak.*

33. *By holding to the impression of the Void (shunya), it is realized that the impression of existence is nothing at all; and, afterwards, by repetition, even this is discarded.*
34. *When an existence is not accepted of which it may be said that it does not exist, then, nonexistence is without foundation: How again can it stand before the mind? As when neither existence nor nonexistence is presented*
35. *again to the mind, then, through lack of any other ability, that which is without support becomes tranquil.*

The different schools had different doubts, and this is also very much the case with ourselves. Because we have doubts, the teachings are in the form of questions and answers. Here the questions are asked of the Madhyamaka school. Although the Madhyamaka school believes in the nonexistence of all phenomena, that everything that is perceived is like a dream, the question is raised that simply having this knowledge would not help us to overcome everything because, as argued here, like the magician.

So the Madhyamaka school replies to this question that the magician could be attached to the attractive women he has created due to his lack of realization of emptiness. If his understanding is very weak, he consequently becomes attached to the illusory woman. However, if one can really understand the state of emptiness, one cuts through habitual patterns and then such attachment does not occur.

So the discussion between the different schools concludes that unless we have realized emptiness we may not be able to overcome the conflicting emotions which is illustrated by the magician's attachment to the attractive woman he has created.

The next discussion raises the point that if all phenomena were emptiness when one has attained total enlightenment, there is nothing to benefit to seeking enlightenment. This discussion starts begins with verse 35:

36. *As a wishing stone and a wishing tree are the fulfillment of desire, so the Body of the Conqueror is seen because of his discipline and his vow.*
37. *As a snake charmer perishes after having completed a pillar [of healing], even a long time after his perishing it still cures the effect of poison:*
38. *So also the Conqueror-pillar, having been completed by conformity to the Way of Enlightenment, does all that is to be done, even when the Bodhisattva has disappeared.*
39. *How can there be fruits when worship (puja) is made to a being without thought? Because it is taught that the one who stands [the living Buddha] and the one who is extinguished [the Buddha in nirvana] are equal.*

40. And according to the Scripture, fruit is there, whether in the hidden realm
(samvriti) or in the really real (tattvatas). Otherwise, how can it be thought
that worshipping the true Buddha is fruitful?

The questions is if there were no mind, then how could an enlightened
being or Buddha take birth? And if there is no mind, how could he
benefit living beings? If the conceptual mind that wishes does not exist,
how could it benefit living beings.

The reply is Just as wish fulfilling jewels and wish granting trees do
not have a conceptual mind which wants to grant wishes, it is simply
because of their being that they grant wishes. Similarly, by the power of
the prayers of enlightened beings and the sentient beings it is that
sentient beings are benefited.

There is another example which you may know better than I because
I am new to Nepal. Somewhere nearby there is a sacred place, where a
self arising *garuda* image appeared from a stone. This was actually made
by an Indian practitioner known as Shanku. It is said that this garuda can
protect beings from any harm that comes from the *nagas.*[24] Now that
great Indian practitioner has passed away, but still the image of the
garuda is effective in protecting beings from the harms of nagas.
Physically the Indian practitioner is not present here, but his activity is
still benefiting others. Similarly, the Buddha's activity is still occurring
even though the physical form of the Buddha is not here.

Another argument is that if there is no mind then such behaviors as
making offerings would not be of any benefit. Making offerings to the
Buddha when he is actually physically present, and making offerings to
Buddha when he is not physically present are regarded as having equal
value. Therefore we can conclude that the mind is not a substantial, firm,
or concrete thing because if it were, then making offerings would have
greater benefit in the Buddha's presence than in his absence.

The next argument is against the Hinayana school which believes
that practicing emptiness (or the path of the Mahayana) is not necessary
to experience total realization. The question is presented by the
Vaibhashika school starting with stanza 40:

41. But if [it is argued] release is by the teaching of the Four Noble Truths,
what good is teaching of Emptiness? Because, following the Scripture,
there is no Enlightenment except by this path.
42. But [it is argued] the Mahayana is unproven. How is your own Scripture
proven? It is proven because of both of us. It is not proven without you.
43. Whatever reasons make them respected, apply these to the Mahayana. If the

truth of that which is valid to both of us depends upon anyone else, then the Vedas, and the like, are true.

44. If it is thought that there is contention within the Mahayana, abandon your own Scripture because of the contention of your own sectarians with themselves and with others and with other Scriptures.

45. The root of religion is the life of the monk); and for the thought which depends upon props, nirvana is as difficult as the life of the monk is difficult.

46. If release is the result of the destruction of passion, it should occur immediately thereafter; but it is seen that those who are in that state still have the ability to act, although without passion.

47. There is no grasping if craving is controlled, but who is not distressed by this craving which is like confusion?

48. The cause of craving is feeling), yet they [of the Hinayana] are seen to have feeling. The thought which has an object must be attached to some- thing or other.

49. Without the Emptiness the imprisoned thought is reborn again, even after attainment of the stage of unconsciousness. Therefore one should cultivate Emptiness.

50. Whatever has been spoken in a sutra, let that become manifest. If it has been hidden, it should be spoken. Nothing is known which is equal in importance to the honored sutras of the Mahayana.

51. If the wicked is made wholesome by having understood a single thought, how can it be denied that a single sutra is the equal of everything taught by the Conqueror?

52. And whatever was spoken by those led by Mahakasyapa is not denied. How can it be done by one like you, since he has achieved a teaching like that of the Buddha?

53. One remains in the realm of rebirth [our opponents argue] without achieving release from clinging and fear, for the sake of the sorrowful, because of confusion. This [they say] is the fruit of the Void.

54. But this objection does not touch the doctrine of the Void; therefore, the Void is to be cultivated without hesitation.

55. The Void is the opposite of the dark hindrances of passion and of intellect. Why does the one who desires all knowledge not cultivate it at once?

56. The cause of fear is whatever thing that is the birth of sorrow. The Void is the soothing of sorrow, so why should fear There may be fear am anything at all; fear will it be?

Following stanza 43 in the Tibetan text there are another five verses of explanation which are not included in the translation of this text, so Rinpoche believes this textbook is the translation of another edition of the text.

This argument addresses the many questions among some Buddhist students which compare the Mahayana to the Theravada teachings and suggest that the Mahayana are not Buddha's teachings because they developed during the time of Nagarjuna (who lived several hundred years after the Buddha). So if you go through the translation of the root text it might clarify those doubts of questions that arose earlier.

Following this is a discussion of the egolessness of self. This explanation addresses both the Buddhist teaching of selflessness and the nonBuddhists belief of selflessness and begins at verse 56:

56. *The cause of fear is whatever thing that is the birth of sorrow. The Void is the soothing of sorrow, so why should fear arise?*

57. *There may be fear from any quarter whatever if I really am anything at all; but if I am nothing whatever, whose fear will it be?*

58. *I am neither teeth, hair, nails, no bone. Neither am I blood or mucus nor phlegm nor pus nor lymph.*

59. *Neither am I marrow nor perspiration. Neither am I fat nor viscera. Neither am I the hidden intestines, nor am I feces or urine.*

60. *Neither am I meat nor muscle; nor am I heat or breath; nor am I the openings of the body or the six perceptions.*

If we search for the self in every part of our body, we are unable to find the self regardless of where we search.

The next discussion is against the nonBuddhists belief that the self exists within the mind. Before the birth of Shakyamuni Buddha there was a small area next to where the Buddha was born known as the Sakya. There a Brahmin, resting in a state of meditation gained some insight. The teachings from a book which he wrote became known as Samkhya. In that belief, the belief of Samkhya, the self is the mind and mind is permanent, that is, mind exists. Therefore, individuals who indulge in karmic activity, eventually receive the results of this karma proving that mind is real. Samkhya takes the position that the mind is not permanent. For example, we are able to see different colors, let us say first white and then yellow. If the mind were permanent, then the shift in mind from white to yellow would not occur.

61. *If there is consciousness of sound, then sound must always be perceived; for without an object of consciousness, how does one know that by which consciousness is explained?*

62. *If unconscious things are conscious, then consciousness would cling to wood. It is certain that there is no consciousness without an object of consciousness contiguous to it.*

63. *If form gives birth [to consciousness], then why does it not hear? Because*

there is no connection with sound? But then it is not consciousness.

64. *Whatever consists of the perceiving of sound, how is it the perceiving of form? One person is considered both father and son, but it is not really so.*

65. *If there are really light, heat, and darkness (sattva, rajas, and tamas), there is consequently neither son nor father. But one who is intent upon the perceiving of sound does not see their true nature.*

66. *Thus it is perceived by another nature, which is transient, like an actor. If this is really the nature of another, this unity is unprecedented.*

67. *If that other nature is unreal, let its innate nature be explained. If it is the faculty of knowing, then all men are identical,*

68. *and both the conscious and the unconscious are identical, because of their common existence. Insofar as difference is only apparent, what then is the basis of their identity?*

Next we have the argument of the Naiyayika school which it says that the mind is empty. Beginning with verse 68:

69. *The Ego [it is argued] is not unconscious because of [native] unconsciousness, like cloth, and the like, but it is conscious because of union with consciousness. The result is the destruction of unconsciousness.*

70. *But [it is argued] the self is immutable. What then happens to consciousness? Its essence is imagined to be like space: uncreated and unconscious!*

71. *But [it is argued] there is no union of cause (karma) and effect, if not yoked together by the self. When one has perished after creating a cause (karma), whose will the effect be then?*

72. *We two are indeed in agreement that the act and the effect have different supports; but if then it is said that the self has no function, discussion certainly is useless.*

73. *If it is said that the effect is united with the cause, this union is never seen. If it has been taught that the one who acts is the one who enjoys the act, [that would involve] recourse to a unity of the phenomenal series (samtana) .*

74. *The Ego is neither the past nor the future thought, be- cause that is seen not to exist. But if the Ego is the production of thought, when that has disappeared the Ego does not exist*

75. *Just as the stem of a banana tree does not exist when it has been divided into parts, so the Ego likewise has become unreal by being examined reflectively.*

This school believes that mind is not really anything, but rather that mind is an emptiness. So when there is no mind, then there is no work of the mind; when there is no work of the mind, then there is no need of the self. The explanation uses the example of the banana tree. Although this tree seems to be something very firm or solid, if you peel off the trunk of a banana tree, you find nothing there that is firm and is the tree. The discussion here is between the Buddhists and the nonBuddhists. The nonBuddhists are uncomfortable with the idea of no self, so the discussion resumes with verse 75:

76. *It may be thought that because a being cannot be found, there is no one upon whom to bestow compassion; but whatever is done [even] in a state of confusion is because of a purpose.*
77. *Yet if there is no being, whose is the purpose? Truly the effort is illusionary; but because it is for the sake of tranquilizing sorrow, the delusion of purpose is not forbidden.*
78. *Because of the delusion of self, the concept of one's individuality, the cause of sorrow, is increased. Since it is destroyed in no other way, the concept of nonself is preferred.*

The question arises that if there is no self, if there is no "I," then to whom is one developing compassion? The answer to that point is that we are not developing compassion to the self, but rather we are developing compassion to the one who is trapped in delusion. So with that explanation we conclude our discussion on the egolessness of the self.

The Egolessness of Phenomena

In this chapter on perfection of wisdom of *A Guide to a Bodhisattva's Way of Life* it is taught that through meditation we can discover egolessness of the individual. Having discussed the egolessness of self, we are now going to discuss the egolessness of outer phenomena. The nonexistence of phenomena is explained here in four points: contemplation of the body, contemplation of the feelings, contemplation of the mind, and contemplation of phenomena.

Nonexistence of self is the lack of identity of that which we feel strongly as an "I." The nonexistence of phenomena means that nothing material has true substance as an independent identity. Whatever we form attachment to, that is regarded as clinging to the identity of outer phenomena. No phenomena truly exists. This is known as the emptiness of phenomena. Clinging to our physical body is regarded as being attached to the existence of outer phenomena. Even if we believe that only parts of our body exist, that is also regarded as clinging to the existence of outer phenomena. So in general, whether we cling to the body or even just to parts of the body, there is no nature, no substantial entity in either body or limb. That is why we mindfully contemplate the body here with:

79. *The body is not the feet or the legs or the breast. Neither is the body the hips, the belly, the back, nor the arms.*
80. *It is likewise not the hands or the sides or the armpits or the shoulders or any external mark. The body is not the neck or the head. What then is the body?*
81. *If the body finds itself partially in all [parts], the parts find themselves in parts, and so where does the body itself abide?*
82. *If the body is everywhere completely in every part, then there must exist as many bodies as there are parts.*
83. *The body is neither within nor without. How is the body in its parts? How is it outside its parts? How indeed does it exist?*
84. *The body does not exist, but because of delusion there is a body-idea in its parts: because of a kind of fabrication, like imagining a man in a stump.*
85. *As long as there is a complete collection of causes, the body is taken to be a man. Likewise, as long as it is in its members, the body is seen there.*

Being discussed that what we think of as a single body is, in fact, an accumulation of many small particles. There is no permanent, concrete entity that is a body. So the body is explained as the accumulation of many particles, just as at a distance a pile of many small stones can be mistaken for a large body or a single form. Similarly, the union of many organs and limbs cause us to think that we have a body.

Not only is the whole body nonexistent, but also the parts of the body are also nonexistent:

85. *As long as there is a complete collection of causes, the body is taken to be a man. Likewise, as long as it is in its members, the body is seen there.*
86. *In the same way there can be no foot, because that is a mass of toes. The limb is likewise a collection of limbs, separated according to their parts.*
87. *The parts also are split into atoms. The atom also is in six sections. The six sections are empty space without parts. Consequently there is no atom.*

Stage by stage we go through the process of proving the nonexistence of the parts of the body. We begin with the hand and go deeper to find that even the nails and the fingers do not exist except as accumulations of small particles. Even the atoms themselves have no ultimate existence.

So, whatever we cling to in the phenomenal world as having true existence can be proven by analytical means not to exist. The next verse explains that with this understanding that there is no identity or existence in anything, we can overcome any disturbing emotion, such as attachment.

88. When the form is like a dream, then who will deliberately fall in love with it? And since there is no body, then what is a woman? And what is a man?

Contemplation of the physical body as we just did now is a method for achieving a gross level of understanding of nonexistence. But having come to an understanding that the body has no independent existence, we still tend to have the feeling that phenomena exists, even though we intellectually realize that the body does not exist.

Nonexistence of Feeling

The next stage is to contemplate is the nature of feeling:

89. If sorrow really does exist, why does it not oppress the joyful? If happiness is dainty food, why does it not please those involved in present grief?

90. If happiness is not experienced, because it is surpassed by something more powerful, what kind of a sensation is it when the essence is not experienced?

91. If sorrow is a subtle state which is destroyed by that which is gross, is it not possible that the other state is a degree of satisfaction? It follows that satisfaction is also a subtle state.

92. If sorrow does not arise in the presence of a contrary cause, then what is called "sensation" has arisen only because of adherence to a fiction.

93. This examination has for this very reason been its antidote. The food of the yogis is that contemplation which has arisen in the field of imagination.

So here we explore the lack of essential nature in feelings. Feeling itself is really mental projection, with no truth or reality in itself. The feeling we experience is what we mentally name as pleasure or pain. For example, when we are happy we enjoy eating nutritious food. But when we are depressed or disappointed, the same delicious food does not give us joy at all. So the feeling of pain or pleasure is a mental projection.

Next is an explanation of the nonexistence of the causal condition for feeling which is explained using the example of the sense of touch. The causal condition of an experience of the feeling of touch occurs through contact between the person and object. But examining this contact we find that there is no contact and no object of meeting.

94. If there is an interval between the sense and its object, how is there a contact between them? If there is no interval, they are a unity; and how then is there a contact?

95. *There is no entering into an atom by an atom; it is equal [to the other atom] and without free space. Without entering there is no mingling, there is no contact.*

96. *How can contact really arise from that which is without parts? And if that without parts has been seen in contact, let it be indicated.*

97. *Contact cannot be made without consciousness, which is formless, nor with an aggregate [of parts], because of its unreality, as previously demonstrated.*

98. *If this contact is not in existence, how is it the origin of sensation? For the sake of what is this effort? Of what is the binding and why should it be?*

So the causal condition of feeling happens from contact of the mind with outer phenomena or the material world. How can that be possible when the mind is nonexistent? How can the nonexistent mind, simple awareness, meet or contact the material world?

Next we have the explanation that there is no person who experiences feeling. So through examining and reasoning, we cannot find the true essence of feelings.

99. *Since there is not seen a knower nor any kind of sensation, O thirst! beholding this situation, why are you not split asunder?*

The next three verses offer a further explanation of how one comes to realize the nonexistence of feeling.

100. *Sensation is seen and it is touched, but by thought [only], which itself is like the sleep of maya Because of its very nature, due to that thought, sensation is not seen.*

101. *In this birth neither that which was before nor that which will be afterwards is remembered or perceived. It does not perceive itself, nor is it perceived by another*

102. *There is not a knower, therefore there is not really any sensation. Since this bundle is composed of nothing, how can one be oppressed by it?*

The Nonexistence of Mind

Having gone through the stage by stage process of examining outer phenomena, we begin to believe that feeling exists. Then we examined these feelings and find that feelings do not exist either. Now we contemplate the mind itself beginning with the next verses in which the nonexistence of mind is introduced:

103. The mind is not in the senses, or in shapes, or within. Thought, also, is not grasped inside or outside or anywhere else.

104.Whatever is not the body and not otherwise not combined and not isolated—what is it? It is because of this that beings are by nature completely in nirvana.

When we examine the mind, we find that the mind does not really exist. We find that the mind cannot abide in the outer realm, the inner realm, or in between. In the next two verse we find that mind was never born.

105. If knowledge is prior to that which is known, what is its original support? If knowledge is simultaneous with that which is known, what is its original support?

106. Likewise, if it should be subsequent to that which is known, then from where can knowledge come? And so the arising of all momentary impressions (dharmas) is impossible.

107A. Since the object would have ceased by the time the consciousness arose, the consciousness would have no object.

If the mind does not exist what causes us to experience consciousness? For example, an object is blue. The experience of being conscious of something that is blue is very much a momentary experience lasting only is an instant. That consciousness of the blueness of the object could not be experienced before you saw the object. You could not have experienced the blueness without perceiving the object, without having seen the blue at all. Nor could that experience of being blue have risen simultaneously, at the same time as experiencing the object. Therefore there was no independent reality in the independent experiencer or in the object. It does not exist as an independent process.

Having contemplated the body, feeling, and mind, we now conclude that all dharmas, all external phenomena have no reality. This is the position of the nonexistence of all outer phenomena made in the second half of 107:

107. If, in this way, there is nothing hidden, then why two truths? or rather, if something is hidden, why are beings released?

Next we will discuss the rejection of these arguments, beginning with stanza 108:

107. If, in this way, there is nothing hidden, then why two truths? or rather, if something is hidden, why are beings released?

108. The one [who is released] is the imagination of another's thought; but he does not exist because of being hidden. He is arrived at afterwards. Likewise, if he does not exist, his hiddenness does not exist.

109. The imagination and the thing imagined are both mutually dependent. Thus it is said that all examination is dependent upon the prearranged.

110. But if that to be examined is examined by what is already examined, then there is no validity to that examination by what is already examined.

111. When what is to be examined has been examined by what is examined, it has no foundation. Because of no foundation, it does not arise, and this is called nirvana

112. But they for whom this is truth are in a perpetually bad position. If an object is dependent upon knowledge, what has become of the reality of knowledge?

113. Likewise, if knowledge is dependent upon that which is to be known, what has become of the reality of that which is to be known? Because of mutual dependence, the reality of both is nullified.

114. If there is no father without a son, what is the origin of the son? If there is no son, the father does not exist. Thus the nonreality of both of them.

115. The plant is born from the seed, and the seed is indicated by it: Why is it not understood that [so-called] reality has arisen only by means of knowing that which is [thought to be] knowable?

116. From the plant it is understood that there exists a seed; from knowledge, the contrary. Whence the idea of the existence of knowledge, by means of which whatever is to be known is known?

This argument asks the following questions: if we practice the mindfulness of body and if the body doesn't exist, what is it that we practice? Likewise if a feeling does not exist, what it is that we feel? And further, if the mind does not exist, what is consciousness? The response to these questions is that the body, feelings, and mind exist at the relative level, but in the absolute or ultimate level there is no essence, no reality to body, feeling, mind, and therefore they do not truly exist.

Emptiness

The next section argues that everything as emptiness (Skt. *shunyata*). The explanation examines cause, result, and essence. If we examine the cause, everything can be viewed as emptiness; if we examine the result, everything can also be established as emptiness, and if we analyze the essence or nature, everything can established as emptiness. This argument is explained in stanza 117 and 118 and refers to the beliefs held by some nonBuddhists that everything is born without a cause.

117. The world, by merely visible perception, regards causation as universal. From a variety of causes arises the variety of the lotus, its stalk and the like.

118. And what has made this variety of cause? The variety of antecedent cause. And why does cause produce effect? The efficacy of the antecedent cause.

These points disagree with the belief that all the substantial material that exists takes shape without any cause. One school[25] believed qualities such as the roundness of a pea or the sharpness of the thorn occurs without cause. The argument against this is that since there is no cause there is also no result. Things cannot go out of existence just like a heap of ash is blown away in the wind, with no essence or result left behind.

There are other nonBuddhists[26] who believe in a creator of all things, a great being such as Shiva. These are refuted in verse below:

119. The Lord is the cause of the world? Then explain who is the Lord. If he is the elements, let it be so. What pains are bestowed upon a mere name!

120. But the earth and the other [elements] are not the Lord. They are multiple; some are transient and without activity and ungodly; they may even be neglected and they are impure.

121. The Lord is not space, because it is without activity. He is not atman, as already refuted. If he is unknowable, then as creator he is also unknowable. What can be said of him?

122. And what does he desire to create? If the atman is it not eternal? The earth, and so forth? It is self-existent. A deity? The same. Knowledge? Without beginning: It proceeds from the knowable.

123. Likewise, happiness and sorrow are from action. Tell what is made by him? For if there is no beginning of causation how can there be a beginning of effect?

124. Why does he not always act? For he is not dependent upon another, because there is nothing which is not made by him. Why is he dependent upon it?

125. If he is dependent upon the totality of things, then the Lord is not its cause. The Lord is not able to act when the totality is complete; and yet he cannot act when it is nonexistent.

126. If the Lord acts without desire it follows that he is dependent. If he has desire he is likewise dependent upon that desire. When he acts, where is the quality of Lordliness?

So the explanation of those who believe the causes were caused by the superior power, really contradicts their own beliefs.

Next is also the tradition of another nonBuddhists known as Samkhya. They believe that everything exist due to the existence of self or "I." That starts in the second half of verse 126:

127. *Those who say that atoms are eternal already have been refuted. The Samkhyas seek primary matter (pradhana) as the eternal cause of the world.*

128. *They teach that primary matter is the equilibrium of the natural qualities (guna), thought to be light, heat, and darkness (sattva, rains, tamas). The world is said to exist because of their equilibrium.*

129. *That which by its own nature is threefold is not a unity. Because of this, such unity does not exist. Even the gunas are not perceived, since they are each threefold.*

130. *Since the gunas do not exist, the existence of sound and so forth, is very remote. It is an impossibility that pleasure, and so forth, is to be found in an unconscious object such as clothing.*

131. *If [it is argued] forms are the cause of things, the existence of things certainly has been refuted. Moreover, your cause is pleasure; it follows that it is not clothing and the like.*

132. *But if pleasure is [derived from such things as] clothing, then pleasure is nonexistent when clothing is nonexistent. Things of pleasure are never obtained eternally by anyone.*

133. *If pleasure is always in the developed state [of the gunas] why is there no perception of it? If it changes to the subtle state, how can it be both gross and subtle?*

134. *Having abandoned the gross, it becomes subtle. Whether gross or subtle, it is impermanent. Why do you not desire the impermanence of all that exists?*

135. *If the gross is not different from pleasure, it is clear that pleasure is impermanent. If it is thought that nothing can arise from nonexistence, because it is nonexistent,*

136. *still you admit reluctantly the arising of that which is manifest, but non-existent. If the effect is contained in the cause, then the one who eats, consumes excrement.*

137. *Also, for the price of the garment, one has bought the seed of the cotton-tree, without wearing it. If because of delusion (moha) the world does not see it, your wise man likewise stands in the same position.*

138. *If the faculty of knowing belongs to the world, why does it not see? Manifest appearance is nonexistent, but it is this which constitutes the world's criterion of proof (pramana).*

139. *Yet if this criterion of proof is not criterion of proof, then what is understood is false. It follows, in fact, that the Emptiness of creatures does not arise.*

140. *If it is assumed that existence is intangible, then nonexistence cannot be conceived. It follows that if whatever exists is false, then nonexistence is*

certainly false.

So the tradition the Samkhyas believe that there is no such thing as cause and effect, both the cause and the result is developed from one, so that cause and effect is happening not from anything other than whatever it is, from itself.

Having examined the cause, our attention now shifts to the analysis of the nature of phenomena. This is dealt with in Stanza 141 and deals with analyzing or examining the nature, so that starts with:

141. *It follows that when in a dream one's son is destroyed, he is not thought to be an object of imagination. The false assumption which has arisen eliminates his existence, which is also false.*

142. *It thus follows from this examination that there is nothing whatever without causation and there is likewise nothing contained in causes, whether in their totality or in their parts.*

143. *Nothing is otherwise perceived, whether it remains or it goes. What is the difference between this [world of causation] and a creation of magic which the stupid consider to be reality?*

144. *Whatever is fabricated by illusion and whatever is fabricated by causes, where does it come from? and where does it go? Thus reflect!*

145. *Whatever is seen because of the proximity of something else, that is unreal. When it is as artificial as a reflection, how is it real?*

Or Batchelor translates it as:

An (effect) will only been seen because of (a cause),
but without (that cause it will) not.
(Since it is a) product,
it is similar to a reflection (in a mirror),
How can it have true existence?

Therefore everything exists in a state of interdependence. One thing cannot exist without another. For example, if we have three squares of wood and stand them up together, leaning on each other, their ability to stand is not with one particular square but rather it is from the interdependence of all three leaning upon each other.

Having examined the arguments on creation and on the nature of things, we next examine the analysis of result with:

146. *When something is existent, what use is a cause? Likewise, when it is nonexistent, what use is a cause?*

147. Even thousands of millions of eons can cause no change in nonbeing. How can anything in that state exist? Or how can that which is nonbeing come to a state of being?

148. If being does not exist in the time of nonbeing, when will it become being? Indeed, that nonbeing will not disappear as long as being is in a state of not being born.

149. And when nonbeing has not disappeared, there is no possible opportunity for being. And being does not go into a state of nonbeing, a state of adherence to two natures.

150. Thus there is no cessation, and there is never being; and likewise, all this world neither is produced nor destroyed.

151. When one investigates, metempsychosis is like a dream—the same as the banana tree. There is no difference between those who are liberated and those who are not liberated.

Here it is explained that from either exploring the cause or the result everything is found to be empty of independent existence.

The text goes on to describe the benefits of realizing emptiness beginning at Stanza 151 to end of the chapter:

152. Since momentary impressions thus are empty, what can be obtained? What can be lost? Who will be honored or despised? And by whom?

153. From whence comes happiness or sorrow? What is pleasant? And what is not pleasant? What is craving? Where is this craving really to be sought?

154. When one investigates, what is the world of the living? Who really will die there? Who will be? Who has been? Who is a relation? Who is a friend? and of whom?

155. Let my companions accept all as resembling space. Because of quarrels and merriment, they are angered, they are made happy;

156. and seeking their own happiness they live, rendering evil to friends, mutually stabbing and breaking, and filled with grief, fatigue, and depression.

157. Dying, they fall into evil places, and experience long and violent tortures. From time to time, after having come to a good place, they become infatuated with pleasure.

158. In existence are many precipices, and yet they are endowed with unreality. There is mutual cessation, and yet there can be nothing endowed with reality.

159 Therein are endless oceans of sorrow, of matchless violence. Therein is a brief period of power. Therein is also the brief duration of your life.

160. Therein is one's span of life uselessly spent in sickness, hunger, fatigue, and toil, in sleep and accidents, in fruitless association with fools.

161. Life passes quickly and in vain, and discrimination is hard to obtain. Whence in those circumstances comes opposition to its repeated perplexity?

162 Therein Mara strives for our fall into great calamity. Therein, because of many evil paths, uncertainty is hard to conquer.

163. And this brief opportunity, the arising of the Buddha, is hard to seize again. Alas! the flow of disturbing emotions is hard to overcome. It is a tradition of sorrow.

164. Alas! exceedingly grievous is the state of those carried by that flood of sorrow, those who do not see their own evil condition and are thus the most miserable.

165. They are like the one who has bathed in fire, yet because he has bathed there, casts himself again and again into the fire. He thinks his condition is pleasurable, and so he makes it even worse.

166 Such persons live for play as if they were undecaying and immortal, and they meet terrible calamities, with death in the lead.

167 When? by means of my own effort, by the arising of a cloud of merit—may I make tranquil those who are distressed in the fires of sorrow?

168. When? by meritorious and zealous deeds for the dispelling of the veiled truth—may I point to the Void those who behold only fantasies?

It is quite easy to talk about the benefits of realizing emptiness. I would rather here like to speak briefly about who is a bodhisattva?

Who is a Bodhisattva?

According to *A Guide to the Bodhisattva's Way of Life* the moment an individual develops the altruistic attitude, bodhichitta, he or she is a bodhisattva. But according to the teachings of Chandrakirti a bodhisattva is one who has reached the first stage of enlightenment, or the first *bodhisattva level* (Skt. *bhumi*). So the term "bodhisattva" is used both on the relative and the absolute level. Traditionally we regard Manjushri, Avalokiteshvara and Maitreya as bodhisattvas. But also on our earth there are many other bodhisattvas. Some appear in the form of great teachers such as lamas, others manifest in the ordinary form of lay men and women on our earth and some even could be manifesting in the form of animals. It is, however, very difficult for ordinary people such as ourselves to distinguish who is and who is not a bodhisattva.

Nagarjuna taught that beings are like the mango fruit. Sometimes from the outward appearance a mango may seem unripe, when on the inside it is totally ripened. And there are times when the mango looks ripe on the outside and is ripe on the inside also. Similarly, we cannot really judge human beings as to what they are. Some people behave pleasantly and their conduct seems to be very gentle, yet inwardly they may not be truly gentle. Others may be outwardly harsh, but their mind could be very gentle. And some might be outwardly gentle and have a gentle attitude within. The Buddha said that only an enlightened person could judge a bodhisattva. So I can only be sure of myself; I cannot judge or decide about others. *A Guide to the Bodhisattva's Way of Life* teaches how to conduct oneself in according with the bodhisattva actions and therefore really enter into bodhisattva activity.

The way to behave as a bodhisattva is to practice the six paramitas. The six paramitas are discussed in the text, beginning with the perfection of generosity, as described in the second chapter about making offerings and again in the tenth chapter as the act of dedication. In the fourth and fifth chapters, the perfection of moral discipline is explained: how to conduct our body, speech, and mind with proper discipline. The perfection of patience is explained in the sixth chapter and the perfection of diligence is explained in chapter seven. In Chapter eight the perfection of meditative stability is explained. Finally the perfection of wisdom is explained in chapter nine.

Questions

Question: Could you please elaborate on the difference between prajna and jnana?

Rinpoche: The origin of these terms jnana and prajna are Sanskrit which were translated into *yeshe* and *sherab* respectively in Tibetan. Before the translations of the teachings of the Buddha, jnana was used in Sanskrit simply to mean "understanding." However, the Tibetan scholars translated the term jnana as "understanding very clearly" and to do this they added the syllable *ye* meaning "primordial" to the syllable *she* which means "wisdom" making jnana to mean "total, ultimate, wisdom." They used sherab for prajna which also means "understanding" to denote wisdom developed through reasoning and logic. Incidentally the Sanskrit word prajna has the syllable *pra* which means "extra" and the Tibetan word shrab has the syllable *rab* meaning "highest."

Question: How do these arguments relate to Mahamudra meditation?

Rinpoche: Both the practices of Mahamudra and Dzogchen deal with the essential nature of mind. To understand that essential nature there is no solid thing that we can point to and say "this is the absolute nature of the mind." Since there is no solid thing to point to its nature is emptiness. This is not voidness like space or the sky, because there is the absolute nature of the emptiness is clarity. There is clarity and emptiness as the nature of ones mind. If you understand that the nature of emptiness is clarity logically, then it becomes easier to adjust to this in meditation.

Question: Once we stabilize the realization of emptiness, have we developed prajna or yeshe?

Rinpoche: When we resolve the nature of emptiness, then we are developing prajna. When we bring our experience or realization out of meditation, that experience is jnana.

Question: Can you say more about developing jnana.

Rinpoche: It might be suitable to explain the example. First if an individual is trying to grow a flower, having the seed isn't sufficient. We have to gather many conditions together such as water and warmth and a pot. When we have gathered all these together and planted the seed, then we can experience the joy of the development of the flower. In our practice, one experience cannot lead to realization. We need to accumulate merit, accumulate wisdom and understanding, and having done that, then with devotion and practicing the meditation, the effort to meditate even without realization, along with the accumulations, can lead to the development of jnana.

Question: How would you define consciousness from a Buddhist perspective?

Rinpoche: Generally the sensory consciousnesses arise when your eye is able to see, the ear consciousness arises when you are able to hear, when you taste something it is due to the consciousness of taste and when you touch something it is due to body consciousness. In addition to all those, there are all sorts of emotions and thoughts that you experience and these are known as the mental consciousness. All these six consciousnesses are known as the skandha of consciousness, which is defined as mind. In more detail there are two more consciousnesses—the afflicted consciousness and the alaya or ground consciousness. One should understand that this is a very brief description of the mind.[27]

Question: Aren't these consciousnesses simply sensory organs?

Rinpoche: No. When you are seeing a physical form, the appearance is taking place in the mind, when you hear a sound the actual hearing takes place in mind. The body is simply a channel, a process to experience those, So the nature of the mind and that of the body are really different and are classified differently with the body being outer phenomena and the mind being awareness, an inner thing.

Question: Could you explain further about the magician's attachment to the beautiful woman he has created?

Rinpoche: The main idea here is whether one can overcome the klesha of conflicting emotion. The question here is simply understanding the emptiness of phenomena. We cannot possibly overcome the klesha of attachment if he magician knows that the attractive woman he has created is not real, that it is empty, yet he still develops an attraction to her.

Question: So one may not be able to really overcome the klesha by simply knowing the emptiness of something. In the example, the magician's has not developed the familiarity of meditation of everything being emptiness. When he has absolutely realized that emptiness, then there is not possibility of the klesha arising at all.

Question: What is an *arhat*?

Rinpoche: The arhats have actually subdued the disturbing emotions, that is why they are known in Tibetan as *dag dampa* or "subdued enemies" in Tibetan. However the manner of overcoming, abandoning, eliminating the disturbing emotions is different between arhats and bodhisattvas. Arhats having realized the knowledge that the root of all suffering is clinging to the personal identity so they meditate on the egolessness of self. Bodhisattvas meditate on the knowledge of the emptiness of all phenomena.

Chapter 10

Dedication

When we have produced the roots of goodness through our virtuous practice, it is also possible in this situation to feel ego-clinging and wanting that these roots of goodness to bring personal happiness. But since this is based on ego clinging, it is important to dedicate the roots of goodness so that one lets go of them. Wishing they ripen and benefit all sentient beings. This is why we have the tenth chapter called dedicating for the benefit of others.

There are two aspects to this point: there is dedication and there is making aspiration. So by the root of goodness that arose from the awakening mind and actually being engaged in the activity of the bodhisattvas of training in the six paramitas. By training in this bodhichitta all the roots of virtue should be dedicated. When we dedicate we should think, "I engage in the activity of the bodhisattvas and have given rise to the enlightened attitude because I shall be liberated from suffering. I shall attain enlightenment but since this idea is based on ego clinging it is important to make the dedication to all sentient beings. The roots of goodness have been made so that all sentient beings may become bodhisattvas. We could, of course, dedicate the roots of virtue to ripen in the form of wealth, good health, possessions and pleasures. There's nothing wrong with that in general, but since all these are merely temporary pleasures, we make the dedication to all living beings may begin bodhisattva conduct, which is then the long-term ultimate good.

1. *Whatever benefit is mine from creating this Introduction to the Way of Enlightenment, by it may all beings become ornaments to the Way of Enlightenment.*
2. *Let as many, beings as there are in all places, who are suffering pain of body or of thought, obtain by my merits oceans of happiness and of joy.*
3. *As long as there is rebirth (samsara) may there be no loss of happiness to them in any way. May the world unceasingly obtain the happiness of the Bodhisattva.*

Some aspirations can be fulfilled and some not. For instance, if I wish fro a beautiful flower on my table, there won't be any flower, no matter how long you pray for it. If, on the other hand, there is soil, a pot, some water and some seeds, then there is a good chance that the prayer will be fulfilled.

So it is important that we don't just pray or wish that things may come about by themselves, but we must try to the best of our capabilities to get the conditions for our wishes. We are very limited as sentient beings in samsara by what we can see and perceive, but actually the realm of sentient beings is inconceivable. In all directions (the four directions, the four mid-directions, up and down to make the ten directions) there are sentient beings and wherever there are sentient beings, there are disturbing emotions and suffering. Now we pray that all these sentient beings may be endowed with perfect happiness, continually enjoying this happiness which is beyond the kind of happiness that occurs in samsara, namely, happiness last only for a while. On the contrary, we wish that they remain in perfect happiness from the virtue of my merits.

4. In as many hells as are found in all spheres of the universe, may beings enjoy the happiness and the pleasures of paradise (sukhavati).

5. May those who suffer from cold obtain heat, and may those who suffer from heat be cooled by the oceans of rains produced by the great Bodhisattva-clouds.

6. May the sword-leaf forest of Yama's hell become the majestic forest of Indra's paradise (nandana), and the torturing trees (kutashalmali) be reborn as wishing trees.

7. May the regions of hell become charming, with lakes filled with the perfumes of unbounded lotus, and with the beauty and delightful cries of geese, ducks, cranes, and swans.

8. May the charcoal mound become a heap of jewels. And may the heated earth become a crystal pavement. And may the crushing mountains become celestial mansions filled with Buddhas.

9. May the shower of swords, stones, and burning charcoal be henceforth a flower-rain; and the unceasing battle of swords be afterwards a joyful flower-battle for the sake of sport.

10. May those who are submerged in the burning waters of the river of hell— their skeleton-bodies the color of jasmine, their flesh wholly destroyed-- obtain by the power of my merit, celestial natures and live by the river of heaven with the goddesses

11. May the trembling demons of Yama and the terrible crows and vultures suddenly behold the darkness dispersed; and ask themselves, "Who can illumine with moonlight, begetting happiness and joy on every side?" and having seen flaming Vajrapani coming through the firmament, having beheld freedom from sin and seen distress disappear, may they thus embrace with him.

12. *Let fall a lotus-rain mingled with perfumed waters that even the dwellers of hell may be quieted. Let them wonder, "What is this?" as they are refreshed with happiness. Let Kamalapani appear to the inhabitants of hell.*

13. *Come! Come, quickly! Let fear depart! brothers who were living beings. That Prince with necklaces, the flaming bearer of peace, has descended to us; he at whose gesture all calamity disappears, floods of pleasure arise, the total Awakening mind is born, and also compassion, the mother-refuge of all beings.*

14. *Behold! At the foot of his lotus are the shining diadems of hundreds of gods. At his head, his vision blurred with compassion, there is a rainstorm of many flowers falling from pleasing aerial palaces wherein thousands of feminine divinities sing his praises. Let there resound also, as is proper, the acclamation of those in hell as they behold Manjughosha before them.*

15. *By my merits may those in hell welcome the appearance of clouds of Bodhisattvas; freed from hindrance; headed by Samantabhadra; joyful, cool, sweet-smelling, windy rains.*

16. *Let them quiet the intense agonies and fears of hell. May those dwelling in misfortune be released from their misfortunes.*

There is suffering everywhere in samsara, whether in the higher or lower realms. The text explains in verses 4 to 16 in great detail how the sentient beings suffer in the hell realms and one prays that these miseries in hell may be purified. As many hells as there are in the worlds, may beings in them delight in the joys of contentment in Sukhavati. Verse 15 explains how one prays for the various suffering of hell, such as extensive heat and cold, being pierced, being crushed and so forth.

17. *May the fear vanish which animals have of being eaten by one another. May hungry ghosts become happy beings like the men of the Northern Continent (uttarakuru).*

18. *May ghosts be refreshed; may they be bathed, and always cooled, by the streams of milk trickling from the fingers of the noble Avalokitesvara.*

Next we make an aspiration that suffering in the animal realm may be purified. Animals suffer mainly from being stupid. They also have a lot of fear of being eaten. So now one prays that the suffering of the animal realm may be purified. The dedication for the purification of suffering in the animal real is given in verse 16.

The suffering of the hungry ghosts is mainly starving and thirsting.

So one prays that the hunger and thirst is eased due to drinking milk that falls from the hands of a great bodhisattva. Also may they be cooled, so that their pain in the hungry ghost realm be purified.

19. *May the blind behold forms. May the deaf always hear, and may pregnant women give birth, like Queen Maya [mother of the Buddha] without pain.*

20. *May all have clothes, food and drink, garlands, sandalwood fragrance, ornaments, all that the heart desires, and all that is most advantageous.*

21. *And let the fearful be without fear, and those afflicted with sorrow be the obtainers of joy; and let those distressed be without distress, and at peace.*

22. *Let the sick be well; let all be freed from bondage; let the weak be strong, and thoughts mutually affectionate. May every region be auspicious for those who travel on the road. May everything prosper which will help them get to their homes.*

23. *And may those held back by a sea voyage find fulfillment of their heart's desire. Having peacefully arrived at shore, may they rejoice with their parents.*

24. *May those who have fallen into a trackless waste find themselves encountering a caravan, and may they travel without fatigue and without fear of robbers, tigers, and the like.*

26. *May the gods protect the sleepers, the insane, the heedless, the ones in danger in pestilent forest or the like—the helpless, whether young or old.*

27. *May they be freed from all importunities; possessing faith, wisdom, and compassion; endowed with good appearance and conduct; and always remembering previous births.*

28. *May they have boundless treasures like Gaganagania. May they be free from opposing commitments, without expedients, and grow in dependence upon one's self.*

30. *May beings who have little strength become of great strength. May those who are wretched and deformed become endowed with beautiful form.*

31. *Whoever are women in the world, may they achieve manhood. Let the lowly obtain it and yet let them remain without pride.*

32. *By these my merits may beings everywhere, without exception, having desisted from all evils, always behave in a proper manner;*

32. *not be separated from the Awakening mind; be devoted to the Way of Enlightenment, surrounded by Buddhas, and free from the works of Mara.*

33. *Thus may all beings have unlimited spans of life. May their lives be eternally happy. May even the word "death" perish.*

34. *May all regions be filled with Buddhas and Buddha-sons, and be made enjoyable by parks of wishing trees and by the fascinating sound of the Dharma.*

35. *May the earth be everywhere devoid of gravel and smooth as the hand's palm, pliant, and filled with cat's eye jewels.*

36. *May groups of Bodhisattvas in great assemblies sit in all places. May they*

adorn the surface of the earth with their splendor.

37. *By means of all birds and trees, and even by rays from the sky, may the sound of the Dharma be heard unceasingly by all beings.*

38. *May they eternally be in union with Buddhas and Buddha-sons, and with endless clouds of worship may they reverence the Guru of the World.*

39. *May the god send rain in due season, and the grain be abundant, and the earth be rich, and the king abide in the Dharma*

40. *And may medicinal herbs be powerful; may spells of invocations succeed; may demons (dakinis and raksasas and such) be active in compassion (karuna).*

41. *May no being whatsoever be unhappy, sinful, sick, forsaken, or despised; and none whatsoever wretched or melancholy.*

42. *May the monasteries be prosperous and full of good reading and recitation. May the congregation (sangha) be eternally complete, and the work of the sangha prosper.*

43. *May the monks) be those who attain discrimination and zeal for the discipline. May they meditate with thoughts skillful and freed from all distraction*

44. *May the nuns be accepted, free from quarrels and weariness. Let them observe the entire rule. Thus all may become true mendicants.*

45. *May the ill-behaved be terrified, always devoted to the diminution of evil. Those who would find Buddhahood, may their vows be unbroken.*

46. *May the scholars (pandita) be honored, received, and given alms. Let their lineage be pure; let it be universally known and praised.*

47. *Not suffering the sorrow of existing in an evil state, without painful experience, may living beings obtain the state of Buddhahood by means of a unique and celestial body.*

In verse 47 there is the aspiration to eliminate the suffering in the human realm and to establish human beings in perfect happiness.

Up until this verse we have been praying that ordinary being may enjoy happiness, now in verse 48 we ask that the intentions of the Buddhas and the wishes of the bodhisattvas may be fulfilled. So we make the aspiration that these great bodhisattvas flourish so that many sentient beings may be happy very quickly. We ask that the wishes of the great bodhisattvas may be fulfilled and that the intent of the enlightened ones may be achieved also so that the unconditioned kindness of the buddhas may pervade everywhere. WE also wish that the shravakas, although they don't have the great wish to benefit limitlessly, achieve freedom from suffering. We pray wishing that inferiors or sentient beings may enjoy happiness and also that the wishes and intentions of the great beings also be accomplished.

48. *May all the company of Buddhas be worshipped in all ways by all beings. May they be exceedingly happy with inconceivable Buddha happiness*

49. May that which has been desired by the Bodhisattvas for the sake of the world succeed. Whatever those Lords think, may it be accomplished by beings.

50. In like manner, let Pratyekabuddhas and shravakas be happy, eternally worshipped with respect by gods (devas), antigods (asuras), and men.   -

51. May I obtain the memory of previous births, and may I attain forever the Level of Delight (pramuditabumi), by the help of Manjughosha.

52. In whatever position may I maintain possession of power. In all births may I obtain the total perfume of discrimination.

53. As long as I desire to see and to question him in any way whatever, may I behold without hindrance the Lord Manjughosha.

54. As Manjushri walks in ten directions and to the sky's edge for the furthering of the prosperity of all beings, let my career be like his.

55. As long as the existence of space and as long as the existence of the world, that long let my existence be devoted to the world's sorrows.

56. Whatever the sorrow of the world, may all that ripen in me, and may the world be comforted by all of the glorious Bodhisattvas.

We now make aspirations for our own benefit. We can also translate that as "may I attain full ordination" or until I reach the Joyous Bhumi (the tenth bodhisattva level). May I always have full recall of my life. May I be able to feel renunciation. May I have faith and devotion. May I be able to train mindfully. Once I reach the first level of the joyous one, then at that time there is not much need to make an aspiration because I will know what to do for the good for myself and others. I will naturally recall my lives and so forth. But until then, I make the aspiration that I may have devotion and renunciation and so forth.

What we truly need in order to be successful on the path is knowledge and wakefulness and wisdom that comes about if we are able to behold the face of the bodhisattva Manjushri directly. Then naturally from this our knowledge and wisdom will develop. So I make the wish that whenever I have the slightest doubt, may I be able to see unimpeded the face of the bodhisattva Manjushri. Will my knowledge and wisdom increase. That is the main aspiration.

Then we make the aspiration to enter the true and authentic activity of a bodhisattva. So we pray to be like Manjughosha, a true bodhisattva. Having prayed for the happiness of sentient beings and for us to enter into the activity of the bodhisattvas band to become just like Manjushri who was able to clear away the suffering of sentient beings and able to eradicate any kind of doubt of sentient beings, we make a prayer that the teachings of the Buddha will remain intact.

57. Only medicine for the world's sorrow, cause of all happiness and success, may the teaching [of the Buddha], accompanied by benefit and honor, endure for a long time.

Sentient beings have all kinds of suffering. What is actually the reason that they have to undergo all these different kinds of suffering? The reason is that they do harm to each other, they do not help each other, because they possess an incorrect attitude of self. This incorrect attitude causes them to suffer from what comes from disturbing emotions of pride, jealousy, desire, and, and the root which is this ignorance of ego clinging. What is needed to change this continuous suffering? Sentient beings need to be free of disturbing emotions. What is then capable of truly liberating us from disturbing emotions? Generally, spiritual teachings are needed to free oneself from disturbing emotions and, in particular, the teachings of the completely enlightened one, the Shakamuni Buddha. Then we are definitely able to completely eliminate disturbing emotions and ego clinging. For this reason we pray that the teachings of Buddha may remain and may increase on this earth.

When we practice the teachings, we will be able to depart from suffering permanently and reach liberation and enlightenment which is permanent happiness. This is the relative view. From the ultimate view, we want to live without too much discomfort in this world. The teachings of the Buddha is also advice on how to be kind to each other, how having a hostile attitude towards others is unwholesome, and how ego clinging is bad. So if we are interested in having a little bit of happiness it is of great importance that the teachings of the Buddha remain. Then there is advice on how to behavior in a wholesome way and how to develop a good attitude. Even if we are not able to fully eliminate hostility from hearing the Buddha's teachings, we will be able to reduce our anger and hostility. If we are not able to give rise to great compassion, listening to the teachings of the Buddha will help. So whether it is for ultimate or temporary circumstances, it is important that the teaching of the Buddha remain. Is it that the teachings of the Buddha re merely on medi..uon? No, the teachings of the Buddha contain all kinds of methods for realization so we wish that the entire teachings of the Enlightened One remain intact.

58. I pay homage to Manjughosha a by the favor which makes beautiful the thought. I honor the Good Friend by the favor which he has thus increased.

We now reach the last verse at which point Shantideva prostrates and supplicates Manjughosha through whose kindness that the wholesome mind issues.

The Story of Shantideva

Shantideva was the son of a King. The night before he was supposed to be enthroned as the ruler of the country, he had a dream due to Manjushri where he was the throne where he was supposed to sit on the following day and he saw that Manjushri was sitting on this throne. Manjushri turned to him and said, "If you take your seat here, nothing will work out. This is my throne." Because of this dream, Shantideva gave up the kingdom and took ordination and the blessings of Manjushri entered into him.

When Shantideva had taken ordination, he went to the great monastic university of Nalanda which at this time was and extremely vast and beautiful compound and a great university. the student monks there were all very intelligent and had wonderful spiritual qualities. They were engaged in either studying or in mediation. But Shantideva did not receive any teachings and he didn't appear to be meditating. he just sat there supplicating Manjushri and received his blessing. Because of this the other student began calling him Bhusuku instead of Bikshu (an ordained monk). The joke was *bhu* meant "to eat" and *su* meant "to sleep" and *ku* meant "to urinate."

Then the monks at Nalanda thought that it wasn't right that he stayed in this university and they thought that they should disgrace Shantideva. They couldn't just throw him out so they said to him, "We are all studying hard and we think you should give a teaching. If you are able to teach well, you can stay; if you cannot teach well, you will have to go." Shantideva agreed and everyone was amazed to hear this. The next day they prepared the throne in the courtyard where a lot of people assembled to hear what Bhusuku has to say. When Shantideva appeared, he want right up to the throne and sat on it. Everyone was astonished, thinking him quite bold to sit right on the throne. Shantideva then asked, "Do you want to hear something said before, or do you want something that is new?" Everyone said, "Please tell us something which has not been said before."

Then sitting on the throne, Shantideva gave the entire teaching of the Bodhisattva's Way of Life and sat on the throne until the 37th? verse of the Wisdom chapter when Shantideva began to levitate. He ascended higher and higher into the air, continuing to teach, and his voice could be heard clearly although he ascended so high that he finally vanished out of sight. He taught to the last verse at which point he prostrated to Manjushri.

Books by Thrangu Rinpoche

The Three Vehicles of Buddhist Practice. This book gives an overview of the Hinayana, Mahayana, and Vajrayana as it was practiced in Tibet. Boulder: Namo Buddha Publications, 1998.

The Middle-way Meditation Instructions of Mipham Rinpoche. This great Tibetan scholar who actually stayed for a while with the previous Thrangu Rinpoche at his monastery describes how one develops compassion and then expands this to bodhicitta and eventually develops prajna or wisdom. Boulder: Namo Buddha Publications, 2000.

The Four Foundations of Buddhist Practice. There are four thoughts one should contemplate before practicing precious human birth, impermanence, karma, and the downfalls of samsara. Boulder: Namo Buddha Publications, 2001.

The Open Door to Emptiness. This book goes through in a easy-to-understand way the arguments made to establish that all phenomena are indeed empty. Vancouver: Karme Thekchen Choling, 1997.

The Practice of Tranquillity and Insight. This book is a practical guide to the two types of meditation that form the core of Buddhist spiritual practice. Ithaca: Snow Lion Publications, 1993

Buddha Nature. This book is an overview of the whole concept of Buddha-nature as it is presented in Maitreya's *Uttara Tantra.* Kathamandu: Rangjung Yeshe Publications, 1993.

The King of Samadhi. This book is a commentary on the only sutra of the Buddha which discusses mahamudra meditation. It is also the sutra which predicted the coming of Gampopa. Kathmandu: Rangjung Yeshe Publications, 1994.

The Songs of Naropa. This book tells the story of the life of Naropa and analyzes in detail his famous Summary of Mahamudra which lays out the path of mahamudra meditation by the guru whose succession of students went on to found the Kagyu lineage. Kathmandu: Rangjung Yeshe Publications, 1997.

Transcending Ego: Distinguishing Consciousness from Wisdom. This book, which includes the original text of the Third Karmapa and Thrangu Rinpoche's commentary, describes in detail the eight consciousnesses and how these transform into the five wisdoms at enlightenment. [Soon to be published by Namo Buddha Publications, 2001.]

Notes

1. This text has been translated at least three times into English. First is Marion Matic's translation which was from the Sanskrit. Second is by Stephen Batchelor as Shantideva, *A Guide to the Bodhisattva's Way of Life*. Dharmasala: Library of Tibetan Works and Archives. Third is Wallace and Wallace *A Guide to a Bodhisattva's Way of Life*. The last translation is compares the Tibetan with the Sanskrit and is also the most up to date.

2. Bodhichitta is the desire to help all other sentient beings reach enlightenment and often takes the form of the bodhisattva vow in which one vows to keep on returning life after life until all beings have reached enlightenment. One could say there are two levels of practice: the Hinayana and the Mahayana. In the Hinayana path one strives to reach individual salvation and one does this primarily with sitting meditation of Shamatha and Vipashyana meditation. The ideal is the arhat who has complete control of his thoughts and feelings and sees the emptiness of the mind. In the Mahayana path, one cultivates love and compassion and bodhichitta and tries to help all other beings.

3. Sentient being refers to any animal or any non-visible being such as a ghost that has a mind. It wouldn't refer to plants or rocks.

4. Marion Matrics translated bodhichitta as "Thought of Enlightenment" and to make the book more consistent we changed this to "awakening mind."

5. "Sugata" means having gone to bliss and refers to the Buddha. A "son" is a bodhisattva and is figurative since there are female bodhisattvas.

6. A philosopher's stone which is used in alchemy both in the East and the West is a substance which is able to turn brass, lead, or iron into a valuable metal such as gold and silver. Nagarjuna is said to have financed the building of hundreds of monasteries by using his alchemical powers to turn ordinary substances into gold.

7. Question: What is a Wish-fulfilling jewel? Thrangu Rinpoche: One can supplicate or pray to the wish-fulfilling jewel and it will fulfill whatever one wishes; whatever one wishes will be accomplished. In the text it refers to a precious jewel. This is different from the wish-fulfilling jewel. If one has a precious jewel; one won't be poor any more and that is the meaning of this analogy.

\

8. Tibetan tradition has it that the mind is located in the heart, not in the head as is in the West.

9. Batchelor's translation is:
   And with gladness I rejoice
   In the ocean of virtue from developing an awakening mind
   That wishes all being to be happy,
   As well as in the deed that bring them benefit.

10. The three lower realms are the animal realm, the hungry ghost realm, and the hell realm.

11. A prayer in Buddhism is much different from a prayer in Christianity or Hinduism because Buddhist do not believe in a God or gods. A Buddhist prayer is an aspiration or a wish to make oneself receptive to whatever energy is necessary to progress along the Path.

12. In the preliminary practice or ngondro practice the bodhisattva prayer is:
    Until I reach the essence of enlightenment,
    I take refuge in all the buddhas
    And likewise the dharma
    And in the assembly of bodhisattvas
    Just as buddhas of the past gave rise to bodhichitta,
    Followed the bodhisattva path
    And through progressive training established themselves
    Into the stages of the bodhisattva,
    Likewise, for the benefit of sentient beings
    I, too, will give rise to bodhichitta,
    And train in the bodhisattva path progressively
    As they did, and become proficient.

13. This word has often been translated as awareness, but we prefer the word attentiveness and reserve the word "awareness" for the Tibetan word "*rigpa*."

14. For more information on the eight consciousnesses see Thrangu Rinpoche's *Distinguishing Consciousness from Wisdom*. Boulder: Namo Buddha Publications, 2001.

15. Buddhist believe that the world we see around us—rocks, trees, houses—is an illusion and not the true nature of phenomena, but a relative reality that we share. A modern example would be that scientists tell us that a book with a red cover is not really red because red is just a wavelength of light put out by the molecules in the cover which our eyes (and not dogs, for example) "see as red." Furthermore, the book is really a complex collection of atoms of Carbon, Hydrogen, and Oxygen moving at incredible speed and

some flying off into space and this would be more like its true nature.

16. Primary matter (Skt. *pradhana*, Tib. *spyi gtso*) is postulated by the Sankhya school to be the permanent, underlying material cause or we might say the fundamental building blocks of the universe like atoms of classical Newtonian physics.

17. Thrangu Rinpoche has made this point by giving the example of His Holiness the Sixteenth Karmapa who is shown in the movie *The Lion's Roar*. When this movie was made, the Karmapa was in the last stages of terminal cancer and the nurses and doctors on his cancer ward could not believe that we was happy and laughing even though he was in incredible pain. This was because he was fine, it was the body which was undergoing difficulties.

18. The four ordinary foundations are part of the refuge (prostration) part of the ngondro practice and these have been fully explained in Thrangu Rinpoche's *The Four Foundations of Buddhist Practice*.

19. In other texts Thrangu Rinpoche has described this process in more detail. The sperm and egg come together and this is called combining the white and red drop. Then someone whose mind is in the bardo (the interval between death and the next rebirth) sees the womb and enters it. There is then a complicated process where the mind begins to see itself as a separate individual and this is due to the force of karma and latencies of previous lifetimes.

20. Batchelor's translation is:
    Whatever joy there is in this world.
    All comes from desiring others to be happy,
    And whatever suffering there is in this world
    All comes from desiring myself to be happy.

21. Hunting and being a butcher has always been considered a very bad profession by Buddhist because one is directly killing animals and animals are sentient beings. When eating meat, one is only indirectly leading to the animal's death.

22. In Verses 141 to 151 of the root text, Shantideva actually reverses self and other so it can be rather confusing understanding who is meant.

23. If you disturb the nagas, they will give you a very serious skin disease which can only be relieved by having a lama do a special ceremony appeasing the naga.

24. This was the Carvakas.

25. There were three major Hindu religions that believed in a creator: Shaivism (with Siva as creator), Brahmanism (Brahma as creator), and Vaishnavism (Vishnu as creator).

26. A much more complete explanation of the consciousnesses can be found in Thrangu Rinpoche's *Distinguishing Consciousness from Wisdom*. Boulder: Namo Buddha Publications, 2001.

The Glossary

Abhidharma (Tib. *chö ngön pa*) The Buddhist teachings are often divided into the Tripitaka: the sutras (teachings of the Buddha), the Vinaya (teachings on conduct,) and the Abhidharma which are the analyses of phenomena that exist primarily as a commentarial tradition to the Buddhist teachings. There is not, in fact, an Abhidharma section within the Tibetan collection of the Buddhist teachings.

absolute truth (Skt. *paramartha satya* Tib. *dondam*) There are two truths or views of reality—relative truth which is seeing things as ordinary beings do with the dualism of "I" and "other" and absolute truth, also called ultimate truth, which is transcending duality and seeing things as they are.

afflicted consciousness (Tib. *nyön yid*) The seventh consciousness. See consciousnesses, eight.

aggregates, five (Skt. *skandha*, Tib. *phung po nga*) Literally "heaps," These are the five basic transformations that perceptions undergo when an object is perceived. First is form which includes all sounds, smells, etc. everything that is not thought. The second and third are sensations (pleasant and unpleasant, etc.) and identification. Fourth is mental events which actually include the second and third aggregates. The fifth is ordinary consciousness such as the sensory and mental consciousnesses.

alaya consciousness (Tib. *kun shi nam she*) According to the Yogacara school this is the eighth consciousness and is often called the ground consciousness or store-house consciousness.

arhat (Tib. *dra chom pa*) Accomplished Hinayana practitioners who have eliminated the klesha obscurations. They are the fully realized shravakas and pratyekabuddhas.

Avalokiteshvara (Tib. *Chenrezig*) Deity of compassion. Known as patron deity of Tibet and his mantra is OM MANI PADMA HUNG.

bhagavan An honorific term for the Buddha meaning "blessed lord."

Bhrama A chief god in the form realm.

bhumi (Tib. *sa*) The levels or stages a bodhisattva goes through to reach enlightenment. Also called the bodhisattva levels. Usually comprised of ten levels in the sutra tradition and thirteen in the tantra tradition.

Bodh Gaya A village Northeast India in central Bihar district where the Buddha reached enlightenment under a Bodhi tree.

bodhichitta (Tib. *chang chup chi sem*) Literally, the mind of enlightenment. There are two kinds of bodhichitta: absolute bodhichitta, which is completely awakened mind that sees the emptiness of phenomena, and relative bodhichitta which is the aspiration to practice the six paramitas and free all beings from the suffering of samsara.

bodhisattva (Tib. *chang chup sem pa*) Literally, one who exhibits the mind of enlightenment. Also an individual who has committed him or herself to the Mahayana path of compassion and the practice of the six paramitas to achieve Buddhahood to free all beings from samsara.

bodhisattva levels (Skt. *bhumi,* Tib. *sa*) The levels or stages a bodhisattva goes through to reach enlightenment. These consist of ten levels in the sutra tradition and thirteen in the tantra tradition.

Buddha Shakyamuni (Tib. *shakya tubpa*) The Shakyamuni Buddha, often called the Gautama Buddha, refers to the latest Buddha who lived between 563 and 483 BC.

Buddha-dharma The teachings of the Buddha.

chakravartin (Tib. *korwo gyur wa*) Literally, the turner of the wheel and also called a universal monarch. This is a king who propogates the dharma and starts a new era.

Chandrakirti A seventh century Indian Buddhist scholar of the Madhyamaka school who is best known for founding the Prasangika subschool and writing two treatises on emptiness using logical reasoning.

Chittamatra school (Tib. *sem tsampa*) A school founded by Asanga in the fourth century and is usually translated as the Mind Only School. It is one of the four major schools in the Mahayana tradition and its main tenet (to greatly simplify) is that all phenomena are mental events.

Choro Lüi Gyeltsen (Tib. *lcog ro klu'I rgyal mtshan*) An early translator.

consciousnesses, sensory These are the five sensory consciousnesses of sight, hearing, smell, taste, touch, and body sensation.

consciousnesses, eight (Skt. *vijnana,* Tib. *nam she tsog gye*) These are the five sensory consciousnesses of sight, hearing, smell, taste, touch, and body sensation. Sixth is mental consciousness, seventh is afflicted consciousness, and eighth is ground consciousness.

dharma (Tib. *chö*) This has two main meanings: Any truth such as the sky is blue and secondly, as used in this text, the teachings of the

Buddha (also called buddhadharma).

dharmachakra (Skt. for "wheel of dharma," Tib. *chö chi khor lo*) The Buddha's teachings correspond to three levels: the Hinayana, the Mahayana and the Vajrayana with each set being one turning of the wheel of dharma.

dharmakaya (Tib. *chö ku*) One of the three bodies of Buddhahood. It is enlightenment itself, that is wisdom beyond reference point. See kayas, three.

Dzogchen (Tib., Skt. *mahasandhi*) This is known also as the "great perfection" or atiyoga. It is the highest of the nine yanas according to the Nyingma tradition.

egolessness (Tib. *dag me*) Also called selflessness. There are two kinds of egolessness—the egolessness of other, that is, the emptiness of external phenomena and the egolessness of self, that is, the emptiness of a personal self.

egolessness or selflessness of person (Skt. *pudgalanairatmya*) This doctrine asserts that when one examines or looks for the person, one finds that it is empty. The person does not possess a self (Skt. *atman*, Tib. *bdag-nyid*) as an independent or substantial self. This position is held by most Buddhist schools.

egolesseness or selflessness of phenomena (Skt. *dharma-nairatmya*) This doctrine aserts than not only is there selflessness of person, but when one examines out phenomena, one finds that this external phenomena is also empty, i. e. it does not have an independent or substantial nature. This position is not held by the Hinayana schools, but is put forth by the mahayana schools, particularly the Chittamatra school.

emptiness (Skt. *shunyata* Tib. *tong pa nyi*) Also translated as voidness. The Buddha taught in the second turning of the wheel of dharma that external phenomena and the internal phenomena or concept of self or "I" have no real existence and therefore are "empty."

five sensory consciousnesses These are the sensory consciousnesses of sight, hearing, smell, taste, touch or body sensation.

garuda (Tib. *khyung*) A mythical bird which hatches fully grown.

geshe (Tib.) A scholar who has attained a doctorate in Buddhist studies. This usually takes fifteen to twenty years to attain.

ground consciousness See consciousnesses, eight

Hinayana (Tib. *tek pa chung wa*) Literally, the "lesser vehicle." The term refers to the first teachings of the Buddha which emphasized the careful examination of mind and its confusion. Also known as the

Theravadin path.

Indra (Tib. *brgua byin*) The chief god of the realm of desire and said to reside on the top of Mt. Meru.

jnana (Tib. *yeshe*) Enlightened wisdom which is beyond dualistic thought.

kalpa (Tib. *kalpa,* Skt. *yuga*) An eon which lasts in the order of millions of years.

kayas, three (Tib. *ku sum*) There are three bodies of the Buddha: the nirmanakaya, sambhogakaya and dharmakaya. The dharmakaya, also called the "truth body," is the complete enlightenment or the complete wisdom of the Buddha which is unoriginated wisdom beyond form and manifests in the sambhogakaya and the nirmanakaya. The sambhogakaya, also called the "enjoyment body," manifests only to bodhisattvas. The nirmanakaya, also called the "emanation body," manifests in the world and in this context manifests as the Shakyamuni Buddha.

Kaua Paltseg 9th cent (Tib. ska ba dpal brtsegs) A translator sent to India by Trisong Deutsen.

klesha (Tib. *nyön mong*) The emotional obscurations (in contrast to intellectual obscurations) which are also translated as "poisons." The three main kleshas are (passion or desire or attachment), (aggression or anger); and (ignorance or delusion or aversion). The five kleshas are the three above plus pride and (envy or jealousy).

klesha consciousness (Tib. *nyön yid*) The seventh of the eight consciousnesses. See consciousnesses, eight.

kunzop (Tib.) See relative truth.

lovingkindness (Skt. maitri, Tib. jam pa) This is compassion for oneself and is a prerequisite to compassion for others (Skt. karuna).

Langdarma, king (Tib *glang dar ma*) King of Tibet who rules 901 to 906 C. E. and tried to destroy the Buddhist teachings. He was assassinated by a monk and Buddhism was restored to Tibet.

Madhyamaka (Tib. *u ma*) This is a philosophical school founded by Nagarjuna in the second century. The main principle of this school is proving that everything is empty of self-nature as usually understood using rational reasoning.

Mahamudra (Tib. *cha ja chen po*) Literally means "great seal" or "great symbol." This meditative transmission emphasizes perceiving mind directly rather than through skillful means.

Mahayana (Tib. *tek pa chen po*) Literally, the "great vehicle." These are the teachings of the second turning of the wheel of dharma, which emphasize shunyata, compassion, and universal Buddha-nature.

Maitreya (Tib. *Jampa*) In this work refers to the Bodhisattva Maitreya who lived at the time of the Buddha.

Manjughosha (Tib. *'jam pa'i dbyangs*) Literally, Manjushri, Gentle Voiced One. A form of manjushri who is the embodiment of wisdom.

Manjushri (Tib. *Jampalyang*) A meditational deity representing discriminative awareness (*prajna*). Usually depicted as holding a word in the right hand and scripture in the left.

naga (Tib. *lu*) A water spirit which may take the form of a serpent. It is often the custodian of treasures either texts or actual material treasures under ground.

Nagarjuna (Tib. *ludrup*) An Indian scholar in the second century who founded the Madhyamaka philosophical school which emphasized emptiness.

Nalanda The greatest Buddhist University from the fifth to the tenth century located near modern Rajgir which was the seat of the Mahayana teachings and had many great Buddhist scholars who studied there.

ngondro (Tib. and pronounced "nundro") Tibetan for preliminary practice. One usually begins the Vajrayana path by doing the four preliminary practices which involve about 100,000 refuge prayers and prostrations, 100,000 vajrasattva mantras, 100,000 manuala offerings, and 100,000 guru yoga practices.

nirmanakaya (Tib. *tulku*) There are three bodies of the Buddha and the nirmanakaya or "emanation body" manifests in the world and in this context manifests as the shakyamuni Buddha. See kayas, three.

nirvana (Tib. *nyangde*) Literally, "extinguished." Individuals live in samsara and with spiritual practice can attain a state of enlightenment in which all false ideas and conflicting emotions have been extinguished. This is called nirvana.

Padmasambhava (Tib. *Guru Rinpoche*) He was invited to Tibet in the ninth century AD and is known for pacifying the nonBuddhist forces and founding the Nyingma lineage.

paramitas See perfections.

perfections, six (Tib. *parol tu chinpa*) Sanskrit for "perfections" and the Tibetan literally means "gone to the other side." These are the six practices of the Mahayana path: Transcendent generosity (dana), transcendent discipline (shila), transcendent patience (kshanti), transcendent exertion (virya), transcendent meditation (dhyana), and transcendent knowledge (prajna). The ten paramitas are these plus aspirational prayer, power, and prajna.

prajna (Tib. *sherab*) In Sanskrit it means "perfect knowledge" and can mean wisdom, understanding, or discrimination. Usually it means the wisdom of seeing things from a high (e.g. non-dualistic) point of view.

pratimoksha vows (Tib. *so sor tar pa*) The vows of not killing, stealing, lying, etc. which are taken by monks and nuns.

pratyekabuddha (Tib. *rang sang gye*) Literally, solitary realizer. A realized Hinayana practitioner who has achieved the knowledge of how it is and variety, but who has not committed him or herself to the bodhisattva path of helping all others.

realms, six realms of samsara (Tib. *rikdruk*) These are the possible types of rebirths for beings in samsara and are: the god realm in which gods have great pride, the asura realm in which the jealous gods try to maintain what they have, the human realm which is the best realm because one has the possibility of achieving enlightenment, the animal realm characterized by stupidity, the hungry ghost realm characterized by great craving, and the hell realm characterized by aggression.

relative truth (Tib. *kun sop*) There are two truths: relative and absolute. Relative truth is the perception of an ordinary (unenlightened) person who sees the world with all his or her projections based on the false belief in self.

Rinchen Zangpo (958-1155 C.E.) A great translator of the second spreading of the dharma (new translation period).

rinpoche (Tib.) Literally, "very precious" and is used as a term of respect for a Tibetan guru.

samadhi (Tib. *tin ne zin*) Also called meditative absorption or one-pointed meditation, this is the highest form of meditation.

samaya (Tib. *dam sig*) The vows or commitments made in the Vajrayana which can be to a teacher or to a practice.

sambhogakaya (Tib. *long ku*) There are three bodies of the Buddha and the sambhogakaya, also called the "enjoyment body," is a realm of the dharmakaya which only manifests to bodhisattvas. See the three kayas.

samsara (Tib. *kor wa*) Conditioned existence of ordinary life in which suffering occurs because one still possesses attachment, aggression, and ignorance. It is contrasted to nirvana.

sangha (Tib. *gen dun*) These are the companions on the path. They may be all the persons on the path or the noble sangha, which are the realized ones.

Shantideva (675-725 C.E.) A great bodhisattva who lived in 7th and 8th century in India known for his two works on the conduct of a bodhisattva.

skandha (Tib. *phung po* Literally "heaps." These are the five basic transformations that perceptions undergo when an object is perceived: form, feeling, perception, formation, and consciousness. First is form which includes all sounds, smells, etc. everything we usually think of as outside the mind. The second and third are sensations (pleasant and unpleasant, etc.) and identification. Fourth is mental events which actually include the second and third aggregates. The fifth is ordinary consciousness such as the sensory and mental consciousnesses.

shravaka (Tib. *nyen thö*) Literally "those who hear" meaning disciples. A type of realized Hinayana practitioner (arhat) who has achieved the realization of the nonexistence of personal self.

stupa (Tib. *chö ten*) A dome shaped monument to the Buddha which often contains relics and remains of the Buddha or great bodhisattvas.

shunyata (Tib. *tong pa nyi*) Usually translated as voidness or emptiness. The Buddha taught in the second turning of the wheel of dharma that external phenomena and internal phenomena or the concept of self or "I" have no real existence and therefore are "empty."

sutra (Tib. *do*) These are the Hinayana and Mahayana texts which are the words of the Buddha. These are often contrasted with the tantras which are the Buddha's Vajrayana teachings and the shastras which are commentaries on the words of the Buddha.

sutra tradition The sutra approach to achieving enlightenment which includes the Hinayana and the Mahayana.

tathagatas (Tib. *dezhin shekpa*) Literally, those who have gone to thusness. A title of the Buddha and bodhisattvas.

Theravadin (Tib. *neten depa*) Specifically a follower of the Theravada school of the Hinayana. Here refers to the first teachings of the Buddha which emphasized the careful examination of mind and its confusion.

three baskets see Tripitaka.

three higher realms See realms, six.

three lower realms. See realms six

Thrisong Deutsen (790-858 C.E.) Was king of Tibet and invited great Indian saints and yogis to Tibet. He also directed construction of

Tibet's first monastery (Samye Ling).

Tripitaka (Tib. *de nö sum*) Literally, the three baskets. There are the sutras (the narrative teachings of the Buddha), the Vinaya (a code for monks and nuns) and the Abhidharma (philosophical background of the dharma).

Vaibhashika school (Tib. *je trak ma wa*) One of the main Hinayana schools. Also called Saravastivadins.

Vajradhara (Tib. *Dorje Chang*) The name of the dharmakaya Buddha. The teachings of the Kagyu lineage came from Vajradhara.

Vajrapani (Tib. *Channa Dorje*) A major bodhisattva said to be lord of the mantra and a major protector of Tibetan Buddhism.

Vajrayana (Tib. *dorje tek pa*) There are three major traditions of Buddhism (Hinayana, Mahayana, Vajrayana) The Vajrayana is based on the tantras and emphasizes the clarity aspect of phenomena and is mainly practiced in Tibet.

Vinaya (Tib. *dul wa*) These are the teachings by the Buddha concerning proper conduct. There are seven main precepts that may be observed by lay persons and 125 or 320 to be observed by monks and nuns.

wish-fulfilling jewel (Tib. *yid shin norbu*) A jewel said to exist in the naga or deva realms which gave the owner whatever he or she wanted. Now used mostly metaphorically.

Glossary of Tibetan Terms

cha ja chen po	phyag rgya chen po	Mahamudra
chang chup chi sem	byang chup kyi sems	bodhichitta
chang chup sem pa	byang chup sems dpa	bodhisattva
Chenresig	spyan ras gzigs	Avalokiteshvara
cho chi khor lo	chos kyi 'khor lo	dharmacakra
cho	chos	dharma
cho ku	chos sku	dharmakaya
cho ten	mchod rten	stupa
chö ngön pa	chos mngon pa	abhidharma
dag dempa	dgra bcom pa	arhat
dam sig	dam tshig	samaya
de no sum	sde snod gsum	Tripitaka
dezhin shekpa	de bzhin gshegs pa	tathagata
do	mdo	sutra
dondam	don dam	absolute truth
Dorje Chang	rdo rje 'chang	vajradhara
dorje tek pa	rdo rje theg pa	Vajrayana
dul wa	'dul ba	Vinaya
Dzogchen	rdzogs chen	Dzogchen
gen dun	dge 'dun	sangha
Guru Rinpoche	gu ru rin po che	Padmasambhava
Jampa	byams pa	Maitrya
Jampalyang	'jam dbyangs	Manjusri
je trak ma wa	bye brag smra ba	Vaibhasika
kalpa	bskal pa	kalpa
khyung	khyung	garuda
kor wa	'khor ba	samsara
koro gyur wa	'khor los bsgyur ba	cakravartin
ku sum	sku gsum	three kayas
kun shi nam she	kun gzhi' rnam shes	alaya conscious.
kun zop	kun rdzob	relative truth
long ku	longs sku	sambhogakaya
lu	klu	naga
ludrup	klu sgrub	Nagarjuna
neten depa	gnas brtan pa' sde pa	Theravadin
ngondro	sngon 'gro	preliminary pract.
nyangde	myang 'das	nirvana

nyen tho	nyan thos	Sravaka
nyon mong	nyon mongs	distrubing emotion
phung po	phung po nga	aggregrates five
rang sang gye	rang sangs rgyas	pratyekabuddha
rigpa	rig pa	knowledge
rinpoche	rin po che	precious one
sa	sa	bodhisattva level
sem tsampa	sems tsam pa	Chittamatra
sherab	shes rab	prajna
so sor tar pa	sor sor thar pa	pratimoksa
tek pa chen po	theg pa chen po	Mahayana
tek pa chung wa	theg pa chung ba	Hinayana
tin ne zin	ting nge 'dzin	samadhi
tong pa nyi	strog pa nyid	emptiness
tulku	sprul sku	nirmanakaya
u ma	dbu ma	Madhyamaka
yeshe	ye shes	jnana

Bibliography

SUTRAS

Gandavyuha sutra (Tib. *sdong po bkod pa*) Has not been translated into English.

The King of Samadhi sutra. (Skt. *Samadhi raja sutra)*
This is one of the few teachings of the Buddha that discusses mahamudra meditation. The first four chapters of this sutra has been translated by John Rockwell at Naropa Institute and the eleventh chapter was translated by Mark Tatz in his Ph.D. thesis at the University of Washington. Thrangu Rinpoche has given an extensive commentary on this sutra in the *King of Samadhi*. Boudhanath, Nepal: Rangjung Yeshe Publications, 1994.

OTHER WORKS

Shantideva

A Guide to the Bodhisattva' s Way of Life (Skt. *Bodhicaryavatara*, Tib. *byang chub sems dpa'i spyod pa la 'jug pa)* Translated by Steven Batcheleor as *A Guide to the Bodhisattva' s Way of Life* Dharmasala: Library of Tibetan Works and Archives, 1982.
The Way of the Bodhisattva (Padmakara Translation Group. Boston: Shambhala Publications, 1997. This is more literal translation of the Tibetan text.
A Guide to the Bodhisattva Way of Life (Wallace, Vesna and Alan. Ithaca, NY: Snow Lion Publications, 1997). This text looks at the Sanskrit and Tibetan and points out where the two versions differ from each other.

Rangjung Dorje

Differentiating Consciousness and Wisdom (Tib. *rnam shes ye shes 'byed pa*, Pronounced *Namshe Yeshe Gepa*) by the Third Karmapa.
This text is a text in Buddhist psychology and was written to describe the eight consciousnesses and how these translate into the five wisdom upon attaining enlightenment. The text and a

commentary is available in Thrangu Rinpoche's *The Treatise Differentiating Consciousness and Wisdom,* Namo Buddha Publications.

Thrangu Rinpoche

Four Foundations of Buddhist Practice. Boulder: Namo Buddha Publications, 2001. This book describes in detail the four ordinary foundations or "thoughts that turn the mind towards dharma" which are precious human birth, impermanence, karma, and the faults of samsara. Besides relating these to one's practice, the book includes Pema Karpo's Practical Guide to Meditation.

Looking Directly at Mind: The Moonlight of Mahamudra Boulder: Namo Buddha Publications,2001. Thrangu Rinpoche gives an extensive commentary on Tashi Namgyal's The Moonlight of Mahamudra which is one of the most comprehensive books on this topic written by an accomplished meditator of this practice as well as a great scholar.